"You send out letters,
you get back letters,
that's for sure!"

—Lazlo Toth

THE LAZLO LETTERS

The amazing, real-life, actual correspondence of Lazlo Toth, American!

by Don Novello

Workman Publishing,
New York

Library of Congress Cataloging-in-Publication Data

Novello, Don.
The Lazlo letters : the amazing, real-life, actual
correspondence of Lazlo Toth, American! / by Don
Novello.
p.   cm.
ISBN 1-56305-285-7 (paper)
1. United States—Politics and government—1945–
1989—Humor. 2. United States—Social life and
customs—1971—Humor. 3. Novello, Don—Correspondence. I. Title.
E839.5.N65   1992   92-7832
973.92—dc20

Citizen's Seal © 1976 by Dave Sheridan

Workman Publishing Company
708 Broadway
New York, New York 10003

Manufactured in the United States of America
Revised Edition
First printing May 1992
21 20 19 18 17 16 15 14

Dedicated to the men and women of the United States Postal Service.

from:
Lazlo Toth
164 Palm
San Rafael,
Calif.
U.S.A. (The best country)

TO: Lazlo Toth
164 Palm
San Rafael,
California
U.S.A.

PM
2 MAR
1974
SAN RAFAEL CA

EISENHOWER USA

MARCH 2, 1974
THE FIRST DAY OF
THE 10¢ LETTER.
HISTORY!

FOR HISTORY!!!
THE FIRST DAY OF THE 10¢ LETTER,
HELLO OLD CHAP.

STAND BY YOUR PRESIDENT...HE'S THE ONLY ONE WE'VE GOT!!!

POSTAGE DUE

THE LAZLO LETTERS

164 Palm
San Rafael,
California
November 1, 1973

President Richard M. Nixon (the best)
The White House
Washington, D.C.

Dear Mr. President,

Fight! Fight! Fight!

I'm with ya!

                    Sincerely,

                    Laslo Toth

                    Lazlo Toth
                    voting for Richard M. Nixon
                    since 1952!

Your message of support was most encouraging. While it is not possible for me to reply personally to all who have been so thoughtful, I do want you to know that I deeply appreciate hearing from you. With your help, I am confident that we can and will achieve the great goals for America and the world to which this Administration is dedicated.

Richard Nixon

164 Palm
San Rafael,
California
November 2, 1973

Vice President Spiro Agnew
Former Vice President of the U.S.
c/o The White House
Washington, D.C.

Dear Vice President Agnew,

Well, that liberal press did it again! Law
and order doesn't stand a chance against the
printing press.....it's just not fair!

You were the best vice President this country
ever had and they go and treat you like some
ordinary crook! Someday they will see the
true light.

Don't forget that there are a lot of people
like me who will always stand up for you no
matter what the history books may say. And
someday everyone will see that you were right!

                    Your friend,

                    Lazlo Toth

                    Lazlo Toth

November 21, 1973

Dear Mr. Toth:

    Your support and encouragement meant
a great deal to me.

    I can only reaffirm my innocence to
you and hope, in this complex and confusing
situation, that you will try to understand
that I believe the actions I have taken are
in the best interest of the Nation.

                    Sincerely,

                    Spiro T. Agnew

164 Palm
San Rafael, California
January 31, 1974

Vice President Gerald Ford
Vice President of the United States
Office of the Vice President
Washington, D.C.

Dear Vice President Ford,

    I was a vice president of a lot of organizations
myself so I know how you feel.

    Keep up the good work! Stand by our country!

Yours,

Laslo Toth

Lazlo Toth

THE VICE PRESIDENT

WASHINGTON

February 26, 1974

Mr. Lazlo Toth
164 Palm
San Rafael, California 94901

Dear Mr. Toth:

Many thanks for your thoughtful message expressing
your support.

It is reassuring to know your thoughts and to have
your encouragement.

Thanks again and warmest personal regards.

Sincerely,

Gerald R. Ford

GRF:irh

164 Palm
San Rafael,
California
February 4, 1974

Mayor Frank Rizzo
City Hall
Philadelphia, Pennsylvania

Dear Mayor Rizzo,

I have been following your career for some
time and would like to take this opportunity
to express my respect and admiration.

I hope someday you will become Governor of
Pennsylvania - and then, I hope, President
of the United States of America!

We need somebody who believes in Law and Order
and no monkey business and you are that man!

Stand up for our President!

A California Fan,

Lazlo Toth

Lazlo Toth

CITY OF PHILADELPHIA

FRANK L. RIZZO
MAYOR

February 13, 1974

Mr. Laslo Toth
164 Palm
San Rafael, Calif.

Dear Mr. Toth:

Many thanks for the words of encouragement.

It is gratifying to know that you follow my activities and that you are among my strong supporters.

I thought you might enjoy having the enclosed photograph and I hope that I will always live up to your expectations.

Sincerely,

FRANK L. RIZZO

FLR:zmd

Encl.

164 Palm
San Rafael,
California
February 15, 1974

Mr. Rawleigh Warner Jr.
President
Mobil Oil Corporation
150 East 42nd Street
New York, New York

Dear Mr. Warner Jr.,

I would like you to know that many Americans
appreciate all the oil companies have done
for this country and want you to know that
just because the press plays up people complaining, a lot of people know the oil crisis
is not your fault any more than it is our
President's. There just isn't enough oil, why
can't people just understand that?

Don't be discouraged, the American people will
someday see that you were telling the truth!
God bless your people all over the globe!

Stand up for our President!

                    An American,

                    Lazo Toth
                    Lazo Toth

Mobil Oil Corporation

150 EAST 42ND STREET
NEW YORK, NEW YORK 10017

February 28, 1974

Mr. Lazlo Toth
164 Palm
San Rafael, California

Dear Mr. Toth:

Mr. Warner has asked me to thank you for your very gracious note of February 15.

With all the criticism we have been receiving lately from some areas of the public, the press, and the government, it is nice to know that we have support from people like yourself.

Thank you again for writing.

Sincerely,

Thomas J. Fay

TJF/bb

Thomas J. Fay
Manager, Corporate Services

164 Palm
San Rafael,
California
February 16, 1974

Mr. Ray A. Kroc
President
McDonald's
Oak Brook, Illinois

Dear Mr. Kroc,

Recently I was driving to Pasadena, California,
and I saw a billboard for McDonald's that made
me start thinking. It showed an egg McMuffin,
which looked very good, and next to it there
was some jelly. Personally, I think a lot of
people will not like the egg McMuffin with jelly.
It would be like putting jelly on top of eggs!

I think that billboard will make a lot of people
not order an egg McMuffin - even though I know
they don't have to use the jelly if they don't
want to.
It just makes me sad that the egg McMuffin looked
so good and that jelly just goes and spoils the
whole thing.

I write this just as a suggestion since I have
enjoyed your hamburgers and fries so much and I
would hate to see your **fine** organization be hurt
by trying to be nice and giving out jelly, but it
just doesn't go.

                              Sincerely,

                              Lazlo Toth

                              Lazlo Toth

McDonald's

McDonald's Systems, Inc.
McDonald's Plaza
Oak Brook, Illinois 60521

(312) 887-3551
Direct Dial Number

March 4, 1974

Mr. Lazlo Toth
164 Palm
San Rafael, CA

Dear Mr. Toth:

In our Egg McMuffin outdoor billboards we show jelly
next to our newest product for one main reason--we
have found that a lot of our customers take off the
top half of the muffin and eat it separately from
the rest of our Egg McMuffin product. The jelly is
provided to make the top half, when eaten separately,
taste even better.

And, just in case you haven't tried an Egg McMuffin
yet, here's a gift certificate which should go most
of the way to buy you one at your nearby McDonald's.
(We think you'll find it delicious.) Or, you can
use it to buy anything else you might prefer.

Many thanks for your letter to Mr. Kroc--and thank
you for your continued patronage.

Sincerely,

McDONALD'S SYSTEM, INC

Darrough Diamond
National Advertising Manager

DD/lm
cc: Ray Kroc
    Roy Bergold

164 Palm
San Rafael, Calif.
February 18, 1974

Mr. Bubble
Gold Seal Co.
Bismark, N.D.   58501

Dear Gentlemen:

I want you to know first of all that I enjoy your
product. It's always refreshing to spend some time
in the tub with some bubbles.

However, I must confess I am puzzled by some of the
instructions on the box. It says: "KEEP DRY".
How can you use it if you keep it dry?

Thought you'd be interested to know someone like me
caught the mistake.

I thought you'd like to know.

                         Sincerely,

                         Lazlo Toth

                         Lazlo Toth

GOLD SEAL COMPANY

"GLASS WAX" — "MR. BUBBLE" — "SNOWY" BLEACH — "FIREWAX"

HOUSTON OFFICE 10303 Northwest Freeway
Suite 514
Houston, Texas 77018

Area Code 713
681-4673

February 26, 1974

Lazlo Toth
164 Palm
San Rafael, Calif. 94901

Dear Friend:

Thank you for your recent letter regarding "MR BUBBLE", which
has been referred to this Consumer Relations Department for
reply.

We are pleased to know that you enjoy using "MR BUBBLE" and
that you find it refreshing to spend some time in the tub in
a bubble bath.

It is true, we do say on our box: Free Flowing "MR BUBBLE"
must be kept dry. By this statement we mean that the box of
powder should be protected against dampness, such as moisture
in the bathroom if the box is not put away. The box of "MR.
BUBBLE" should be closed and placed in a cabinet until the next
use.

Some people tell us they transfer the "MR BUBBLE" powder to a
plastic container, or even a large coffee can, to keep dampness
out of the powder. Some have mentioned they keep a measuring
scoop in the can for convenient measuring of the proper amount
of powder to use in each bath. Over-use is only wasteful.

Our other products are listed above in our letterhead. We are
enclosing an educational bulletin based on our "SNOWY" BLEACH
which we would appreciate your giving to your mother. Perhaps
you already use "SNOWY" in your home. "SNOWY" is the safe
oxygen-type bleach for all washable fabrics and colorfast dyes.
When regular laundry such as sheets, towels, underwear and linens
are washed with "SNOWY" from the very beginning, and in each wash
load, these items will have stronger fiber strength, longer life
and better appearance than when harsh chlorine bleaches are used.

Thank you again for writing to us.

Yours very truly,
GOLD SEAL COMPANY

M. Hershey,
Consumer Relations Dir.

Encl.
Bulletin #22
"SNOWY" & "MR BUBBLE"
Coupons

164 Palm
San Rafael, Calif.
February 27, 1974

Mr. Sammy Davis Jr.
c/o Mt. Sinai Hospital
Miami, Florida

Dear Mr. Davis Jr.,

Glad to hear that you'll be out of the hospital
soon. Hospitals are terrible places but they
give you a chance to catch up on your jello!
You can use that line - just say that you got it
from me at the end of your act. Just say, "some
of my jokes are by Lazlo Toth", that will be fine.

I also have a lot of political jokes that you can
use. It seems that the only political jokes around
these days are against our President - but all mine
are against the commies. I don't think people should
make fun of our President. After all, he's the only
one we've got!

Are you feeling better? You really had me scared
there when I heard you had chest pains. That
usually means the old ticker - our most valuable
organ. Once the heart goes, that's it!

Why don't you ever sing Candy Man on T.V. anymore?
All we ever get is Wayne Newton. You know what's
good about Wayne Newton? Nothing!
Would you please send me your picture? I was going
to send you some candy but they told me you probably
would just throw it out cause everybody sends you
candy and you have so much you wouldn't know what to
do with it.

Stay true to our President! He needs you now more
than ever!

I've liked you ever since you were in the Little
Rascals.

                              Right on,

                              Lazlo Toth

                              Lazlo Toth

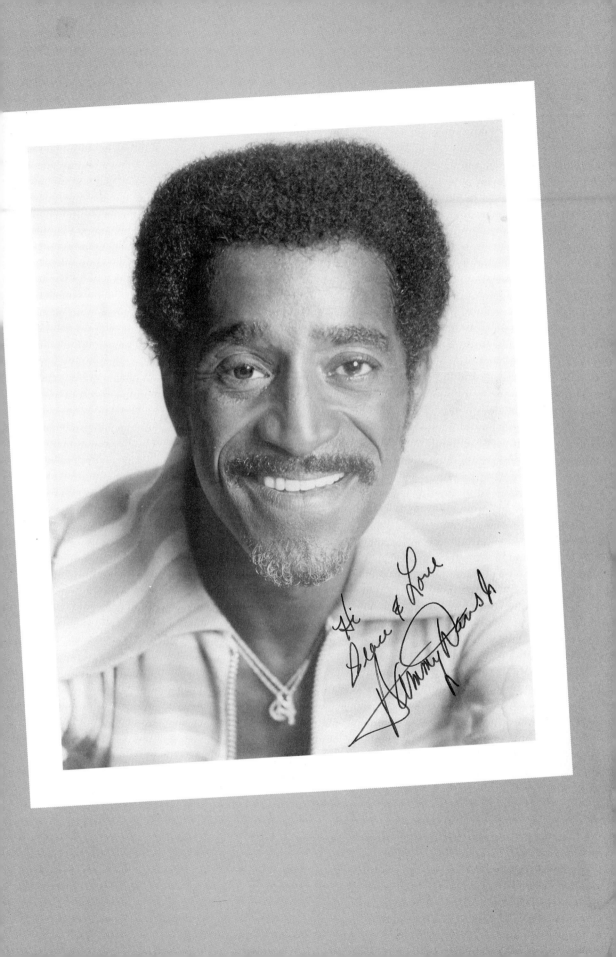

164 Palm
San Rafael,
California
February 28, 1974

Mr. Bebe Rebozo
c/o The White House
Washington, D.C.

Dear Mr. Rebozo,

I have been reading about you quite a lot
in the last few years. Our President needs
a friend like you by his side, and God bless
you for it!

I am writing concerning some revelations I
had while reading the newspapers the last
few days. Concerning the conversation that
our President had with John Dean, I read in
today's paper that he was quoted as saying,
"It is wrong, that's for sure", but in a
Newsweek magazine about a week ago, it quoted
him as saying he said, "There is no problem
raising a million dollars, we can do that,
but it would be wrong."
Did you get it? He forgot to say, "that's
for sure". Please, remind him to say he said
"that's for sure", I think that's where they
are trying to trip him up. I just wanted to
warn him and thought you could tell him for
me - - it's better than a letter to him, I
know how he probably has all his mail read by
spies.

I trust that you will discuss this matter with
him. Remember that as a confidant of our
President you are serving a very important
duty. Stand by our President! And give him
my best wishes!

NO REPLY !   Respectfully,

                                 Lazlo Toth

                                 Lazlo Toth

164 Palm
San Rafael,
California
March 1, 1974

M. Hershey
Consumer Relations Dir.
Gold Seal Company
10303 Northwest Freeway
Houston, Texas 77018-ZIP

Dear M. Hershey,

I was being nice to tell you about the error
you have on your box and you send me coupons
and tell me to give an educational bulletin
about stains to my Mother.

To begin with, I wouldn't give your lousy
educational bulletin #22 to nobody! Everybody I know knows more about stains and that
stuff than your fancy company will ever know!
Why you don't even know how to thank someone
when they offer you an intelligent suggestion!
And then you have the nerve to try to give me
some pitch about your BLEACH!
I was writing about MR. BUBBLE, I don't care
about BLEACH! What does BLEACH have to do
with it? Come on!
And how come the only words in capitals are
your SNOWY BLEACH and MR. BUBBLE while my
Mother doesn't even get a capital for her M!

This is a warning that I'm thinking of moving
on to another bubble bath.

Stand by our President!

                          with a right to be angry,

                          Lazlo Toth

Encl.
Bulletin #22
SNOWY and MR. BUBBLE
Coupons

GOLD SEAL COMPANY

"GLASS WAX" — "MR. BUBBLE" — "SNOWY" BLEACH — "FIREWAX"

HOUSTON OFFICE 10303 Northwest Freeway
Suite 514
Houston, Texas 77018

March 4, 1974

Area Code 713
681-4673

Lazlo Toth
164 Palm
San Rafael, Calif. 94901

Dear Friend:

This is to acknowledge your letter of March 1st and to say that we regret that our reply to your suggestion of February 18th was not satisfactory to you.

We certainly do appreciate your suggestion that we eliminate the words "keep dry" on our "MR BUBBLE" box. As mentioned in our previous letter, we say "keep dry" for important reasons:

> For instance, if the box is left on the side of the tub, it could become wet, and the powder would no longer be free-flowing.

> If the box is left open in a bathroom that has much moisture in the air, the powder could absorb the moisture, and again would not be free-flowing.

Like other manufacturers of products sold in grocery stores and advertised on television, we receive thousands of letters each year, some praising one of our products, some complaining, and others with suggestions. We answer each letter received as courteously as possible, and in almost every instance we mention one of our other products and send some of our advertising. We regret if we offended you in doing so, but assure you this was only a friendly gesture.

Thank you again for your suggestion, and naturally we hope that you will continue to use and enjoy "MR BUBBLE".

Yours very truly,
GOLD SEAL COMPANY

M. Hershey,
Consumer Relations Dir.

MH/

164 Palm
San Rafael,
California
March 1, 1974

Personnel Director
J. Walter Thompson
420 Lexington Avenue
New York, New York

Dear Sir:

I've been reading about your wonderful company
in the newspapers and would like to take this
opportunity to apply for employment.
Although I have never worked in advertising,
I have many of the same traits. (Art is my
business, tape recorder knowledge, etc.)

1. Art Director
2. Media Buyer
3. Account Executive
This can be in any country where you need me.
Not Yugoslavia, Turkey, India or Balkans.

Do you still do the advertising for Listerine?
(My favorite!)

Background
Many of the fine schools furnish the ways to
future employment.

Hoping for a response within the week or longer
if you can't get around to it right away, I'll
understand.

Moving expenses: Who pays? Do we split?

God bless America.
God bless Richard M. Nixon. (the best!)

Sincerely,

Lazlo Toth

P.S.
I have many ideas ready to go.

J. WALTER THOMPSON COMPANY
420 LEXINGTON AVENUE, NEW YORK, N. Y. 10017
686-7000

March 6, 1974

Mr. Lazlo Toth
164 Palm
San Rafael, California

Dear Mr. Toth:

Thank you for your recent inquiry regarding employment
with the J. Walter Thompson Company.

Unfortunately, we have no suitable opening for someone
with your qualifications at the present time.

We will be happy to hold your resume in file, however,
and get in touch with you should the situation change.

Sincerely,

Ms. Leslee Hellman
Creative Administration

LH:dk

164 Palm
San Rafael, Calif.
March 2, 1974

President Richard M. Nixon
President of The United States of America
Washington, D.C.

Dear Mr. President:

I just read in the newspaper where your former chief
of staff, former chief domestic advisor, former attorney
general, former assistant attorney general, former
special counsel, former attorney, and one of your former youthful aides were indicted.
The newspapers would have Americans believe that these
fine public servants are guilty. And they would have
the American people believe, by sly insinuations, that
you are guilty, too.
I think their plan is to keep you involved with this
sordid Watergate affair and keep you away from doing
the real important business of the country.
But, I know you're smarter than to fall for some Eastern
establishment "made you look" strategy.

I have a plan to suggest to you that I think may be our
answer.
What I think we should do is this:
1. Resign in April or May. (Whichever you prefer.)
    This will be a real shock to the Nation and will
    serve the newspapers right. Millions of Americans
    will feel sorry for you and, to be honest, this
    will help. The country will also know what it's
    like to have Ford in there.

then,

2. After "retiring" in Florida for a few months, on
    July 4, 1975, you announce your plans to run for
    President in 1976!
    This will give you _four_ more _great_ years instead
    of _three_ more _mediocre_ years.
    You've got to admit, it makes sense.

I hope you will consider this plan. Otherwise, this
Watergate thing is going to drag on and just sap up all
your valuable energy.

God bless America.
Richard Milhouse Nixon....The Best!

                    Loyally,

                    Lazlo Toth

                    Lazlo Toth
                    voting for Richard M. Nixon
                    since 1952!

Your message of support was most encouraging. While it is not possible for me to reply personally to all who have been so thoughtful, I do want you to know that I deeply appreciate hearing from you. With your help, I am confident that we can and will achieve the great goals for America and the world to which this Administration is dedicated.

Richard Nixon

SUPPORT
LAW
& ORDER

NATIONAL POLICE Venice
HALL OF FAME Florida 35595

164 Palm
San Rafael, Calif.
March 3, 1974

President Ferdinand Marcos
Manila, Philippine Islands

Dear President Marcos,

I have followed your career for quite some
time and would like to take this opportunity
to say, "well done!".

It is "rare" and in some cases "medium rare"
to have someone of your stature in the world
today. Keep it up!

It seems one can't go into an emergency room
in this country without meeting one of your
interns or go into a stationery store without
seeing some of your envelopes. Bravo!
And so, I would like to say, "thank-you" and,
if you're ever in this neck of the planet,
look me up.

Law and order forever!

Send me your picture.

                              Good luck,

                              Lazlo Toth

                              Lazlo Toth

Office of the President
of the Philippines
Malacañang

March 27, 1974

Mr. Lazlo Toth
164 Palm
San Rafael, California
U. S. A.

Dear Mr. Toth:

This is to acknowledge, on behalf of President Marcos, your letter of 3 March 1974, for which the President thanks you.

I am happy to enclose the photograph of the President that you requested.

With all good wishes.

Truly yours,

R. C. TUVERA
Presidential Assistant

Encl. :a. s.

164 Palm
San Rafael, Calif.
U.S.A.
March 4, 1974

President Chung Hee Park
President of South Korea
Seoul, Korea

Dear President:

I have been an admirer of yours for years
and am always interested to hear any news
I can about you.

I just saw in the paper where five novelists
were indicted in Seoul. I'm happy to see
that you are cracking down on literary men.
They are the ones that cause trouble, what
with all their talk of "freedom".

I want you to know that we used to have a
lot of trouble with our students here just
like you do now. But good old law and order
and a few stiff sentences for minor offences
made them quiet down quick. Now they've
grown up and have become responsible tax
paying careerists. Just give them a little
time. Youth always has high ideals. Age
will change them, don't worry.

Best of luck in the future. Send me your
picture, my friend.

                              Respectfully,

                              Lazlo Toth

                              Lazlo Toth

Ch'ong Wa Dae
Seoul, Korea

March 14, 1974

Dear Mr. Toth:

President Park has asked that I write to you thanking for your letter of March 4.

We do appreciate knowing of your deep concern with the developments in Korea, and are sending you herewith a copy of President's picture. Also, we are sending you some up-to-date publications under separate cover, via sea mail, and hope they will help you deepen your understanding of Korea and the Korean people.

Please accept the President's best wishes to you for a happy and prosperous future.

Sincerely,

Sangho Cho
Sangho Cho
Senior Protocol Secretary
to the President

Mr. Lazlo Toth
    164 Palm
        San Rafael, California
            U. S. A.

164 Palm
San Rafael,
California
U.S.A.
March 6, 1974

Generalissimo Francisco Franco
El Presidente of Espana (Spain)
Madrid, Espana (Spain)

Dear Generalissimo,

I have been an admirer of yours for
years and years and years and would
like to take this opportunity to
offer you my respect and admiration.

In this topsy turvy crazy world we
live in, it puts my heart at peace
to know that there is someone like
you - standing like an inorganic rock
of ultraconservatism - in a beautiful
sky we must try a million not to
change! Bravo Generalissimo!

You are not just a general - you are
truly a Generalissimo! Keep it up!

Would you honor me by sending your
picture? It will be my pleasure.
Viva El Generalissimo!
Viva Richard Nixon!

                    Your kind of guy,

                    Lazlo Toth
                    Lazlo Toth

April 26, 1974

Mr. Lazlo Toth
164 Palm,
San Rafael —CALIFORNIA
        (USA)

Dear Mr. Toth,

        In accordance with the request contained
in your letter of March 6th last, addressed to H.E.
the Head of State and Generalissimo, I have pleasure
in enclosing his photograph,
        Yours truly,

Alejandro Royo-Villanova

164 Palm
San Rafael, Calif.
March 6, 1974

Mr. H.R. Haldeman
c/o The White House
Washington, D.C.

Dear Mr. Haldeman,

I have always been a fan of yours and have
always stuck up for you. However, after seeing
you on television last night I was terribly
disappointed.

I believe you are completely innocent but
you are hurting your own image with that long
hair. Just because you lost your job doesn't
mean you shouldn't keep up your appearance!

Maybe if you get a good American flat top like
you used to have our President will find some
other job for you.

I don't mean any disrespect. I just liked you
better before. Didn't you ever hear the saying,
"Don't change boats in the middle of the river"?
The same goes for hair! And yours was so nice!
It reminded me of Tab Hunter.

Best of luck. Stand by our flag!

                              Still a supporter,

                              Lazlo Toth

                              Lazlo Toth

H. R. HALDEMAN
443 NORTH McCADDEN PLACE
LOS ANGELES, CALIFORNIA 90004

May 9, 1974

Mr. Lazlo Toth
164 Palm
San Rafael, California

Dear Mr. Toth:

Thank you very much for your letter of several months
ago. I am sorry to be so long in replying but it
took awhile for the letter to reach me from the White
House.

I am sorry you don't like the TV appearance of my
longer hair but I can assure you that it isn't a
matter of my failing to keep up my appearance
because of having lost my job.

In any event, I deeply appreciate your support and
good wishes and I can assure you I will stand by our
flag as you urge.

Sincerely,

H.R. Haldeman

164 Palm
San Rafael,
California
March 11, 1974

Mr. Dean Burch
Counselor to the President
The White House
Washington, D.C.

Dear Mr. Burch,

Congradulations! I just read that you were
sworn in as a counselor to President Nixon
and as a member of his cabinet.

I understand that you will be advising our
President on matters of politics. Well, he
sure needs you! Things have been pretty
rough for him lately and I think it's wonderful that you're there to help. Some people
would look upon his cabinet as a sinking
boat. But let them remember this: It's the
women and children who get in the life rafts
first. The men remain until last!

Bravo Burch! Bravo Nixon!

"The best is yet to come."
                    - Johnny Mathis

                              Your friend,

                              Lazlo Toth
                              Lazlo Toth

THE WHITE HOUSE

March 18, 1974

Mr. Lazlo Toth
164 Palm
San Rafael, California

Dear Mr. Toth:

Thank you for your letter of March 11, 1974. I
am grateful for your good wishes as I undertake
this new and very challenging assignment.

It is particularly encouraging to know of your
strong support for sound approaches to the
major national issues we face, and I know
that the President would be deeply appreciative.

With every good wish.

Sincerely,

Dean Burch,
Counsellor to the President

164 Palm
San Rafael,
California
March 11, 1974

Ambassador Richard Helms
Ambassador to Iran
The American Embassy
Tehran, Iran (Persia)

Dear Ambassador Helms,

It makes me happy to know that our
country has someone like you repre-
senting us in Iran.

Some people only know about Iran
because of the rugs, but anyone
keeping up with the news knows about
the trouble between Simon and The
Shah and knows it's a hot spot.

I liked you when you were director
of the C.I.A. and when you were on
T.V. standing up for our President.
Keep up the good work!

Congradulations! Carry on!

                          Respectfully,

                          Lazlo Toth

                          Lazlo Toth

EMBASSY OF THE
UNITED STATES OF AMERICA
Tehran, Iran

March 20, 1974

Mr. Lazlo Toth
164 Palm
San Rafael, California

Dear Mr. Toth:

It was most cordial of you to write me as you
did under date of March 11.

Since tomorrow is the Iranian New Year, I take
this occasion to wish you every success in whatever
endeavor you may be engaged. This is in the true
spirit of Now Rouz.

Sincerely yours,

Richard Helms
Ambassador

164 Palm
San Rafael,
California
March 13, 1974

General William Westmoreland
The Republican Party State Headquarters
616 Hardin Street
Columbia, South Carolina

Dear General Westmoreland,

Well, it won't be long and it will be
Governor Westmoreland! Put another
feather in that hat! Congradulations!

Even though the Viet Nam war is over,
I still remember you. Keep up your
knowledge in warfare and you can be
another Ike! We could use another
General in the White House!

The Republican Party sure can use you now!
Fight! Fight! Fight!

Stand by our President! He got us out of
Viet Nam and he gave us China and Russia!
Just because he fibbed a little shouldn't
make people forget all the good he did!
How about his daughters?

                                Good luck,

                                Lazlo Toth
                                Lazlo Toth

23 March 1974

Dear Mr. Toth:

Thank you for your warm note of March 13th. I appreciate your
endorsement of my decision to throw my hat into the political
ring for the Governorship of South Carolina on the Republican
ticket.

I agree with you that Ike made a good President.

                              Sincerely,

                              W. C. WESTMORELAND

Mr. Lazlo Toth
164 Palm
San Rafael, CA

164 Palm
San Rafael,
California
March 13, 1974

Mr. Ray A. Kroc
President
McDonald's
Oak Brook, Illinois

Dear Ray,

I got a letter from Darrough Diamond about
a week ago where he said thanks to me for
writing to you. That's okay, my pleasure.

He explained to me how people don't put
the jelly on top of the egg but eat the top
part separate from the egg part. Pretty
clever! I went and had one like that and
it did make the top half taste even better,
just like he said.

Yesterday, I went over to my Mac place (that's
what I call it, they all know me there) and
I ordered a hamburger and asked for some jelly
and they wouldn't give it to me. I told them
how I was friends with you and all but they
said they only give it out with the Egg Mc-
Muffin. I brought my hamburger home and split
it up and used the top half separate just like
Darrough suggested, but I don't see why I have
to use my own jelly and the Egg McMuffin people
get theirs for free. The top half of the hamburger bun tastes even better like that too.
It's just not fair!

I see where you're up to 10 Billion hamburgers
sold. How many more do you have to go?

Stand by our President!

                              Your friend,

                              Lazlo

                              Lazlo Toth

McDonald's Systems, Inc.
McDonald's Plaza
Oak Brook, Illinois 60521
(312) 887-3551
Direct Dial Number

March 21, 1974

Mr. Lazlo Toth
164 Palm
San Rafael, CA

Dear Mr. Toth:

Glad to know you tried the top half of the Egg
McMuffin product with jelly, and that you liked it.

To your point about giving jelly with hamburgers,
there just aren't many people who like hamburgers
that way. Most people prefer ketchup, mustard,
onions and pickles--the way we make 'em.

Thanks for your note.

Sincerely,

McDONALD'S SYSTEM, INC.

Darrough Diamond
National Advertising Manager

DD/lm
cc: Ray Kroc
     Roy Bergold

```
                              164 Palm
                              San Rafael,
                              California
                              March 17, 1974

          Mayor Richard J. Daley
          Mayor of Chicago
          City Hall
          Chicago, Illinois

          Dear Mayor Daley,

          You can't imagine how I felt when I saw you
          on T.V. (television) holding hands with Rich-
          ard Nixon!
          You are a true patriot - a man who puts love
          of country above party politics in a time of
          need!  God will bless you for it!

          The first time I saw you in person was right
          after the Demo convention in Chicago in 1968.
          You were in Grant Park planting a tree for
          Arbor Day and you said, "If those hippies and
          yippies were here they would plant the little
          tree upside down."
          It was a brilliant speech and you have been
          my number one favorite ever since!

                              Your kind of guy,

                              Lazlo Toth
                              Lazlo Toth
```

OFFICE OF THE MAYOR
CITY OF CHICAGO

RICHARD J. DALEY
MAYOR

March 28, 1974

Dear Mr. Toth:

Many thanks for writing to me about President
Nixon's visit to Chicago. I feel, as you do, that
Richard M. Nixon is President of all the people and
the Presidency should be accorded full respect and
dignity at all times.

With kindest regards,

Sincerely,

Mayor

Mr. Lazlo Toth
164 Palm
San Rafael, California

164 Palm
San Rafael,
California
March 18, 1974

President Richard M. Nixon
President of the U.S.A.
The White House
Washington, D.C.

Dear Mr. President,

I just read in the paper where all the people
at the airport in Nashville stood up and sang
Stand Up and Cheer for Richard Nixon. It
sure sounds like a good song - especially
good to me because they sang it to the tune
of Okie from Muskogee - one of my favorites!
First, I like Birthday Thank You Tommy from
Viet Nam and lately I like The Americans by
a Canadian fellow who talks up for the U.S.
You should give him some kind of medal for
that! It's the greatest thing to happen to
this country since extra crispy chicken! (You
can use that.)

The reason that I wrote was to send you a
song I wrote about you. I like Stand Up and
Cheer for Richard Nixon, don't get me wrong.
This is another one - if you want to do more
than one if your plane is late or something.
It's called Be True To Your President! (To the
tune of Stars and Stripes Forever.)

                    Be True To Your President!
                              by Lazlo Toth

          Be true to your President,
          He's the best that there is
               that's for sure;
          He'll fight for what's right
               never quittin',
          My President, your President,
               Richard Nixon.

I hope you like it. It sounds best if you
kind of march along as you sing it. If someone
wants to record it (not Wayne Newton) I'll
donate all the money I make from it to a charity.
(Whichever one sounds best.) Let me know.

                         Hang in there,

                         Lazlo Toth

                         Lazlo Toth

THE WHITE HOUSE

WASHINGTON

April 4, 1974

Dear Mr. Toth:

The President appreciates your thoughtfulness
in sending him your song. He wants you to
know that he is grateful for your kindness
and you have his best wishes.

Sincerely,

Roland L. Elliott
Special Assistant
to the President

Mr. Lazlo Toth
164 Palm
San Rafael, California 94901

164 Palm
San Rafael,
California
March 18, 1974

President
Kentucky Fried Chicken Corporation
1441 Gardiner Lane
Louisville, Kentucky

Dear Sir:

The Free Enterprise System is in for an attack
that will directly effect your corporation!

It is my American duty to inform you that there
are people in this country who, in the name of
"environmentalists" and "friends of chickens",
are mere dupes of the red menace that is ever
so slowly trying to creep into our very minds.

A group calling itself <u>Changing Times Not Tires</u>,
made up of militant ex-auto mechanics, is de-
manding that America abandon our mascot The American Eagle and adopt a new national bird. They
say, "Extinct birds belong to extinct times".
But the proudest bird that ever lived is not extinct! There are at least two hundred alive in
North America alone!

The C.T.N.T. is pushing for the <u>chicken</u> to become
the new national bird! They say it helped make
this country succeed more than any other bird and
if it sounds like a solid idea to you, you're right.
But if they make the chicken the new national bird,
you're in trouble! Nobody is going to want to eat
the national bird so you'll have to go out of business! I know now you can see the seriousness of
this!

I don't care about chickens - although I eat them.
I only want to keep the eagle our national bird!
It would be to our advantage to keep the eagle as
our symbol and the chicken as our dinner, and by
working together we can do it! God bless you!

I love your potatoes best!

Let me know your ideas on the subject.
Stand by our President!
My best to the Colonel. A wonderful American!

To the Eagle forever,

Lazlo Toth

Kentucky Fried Chicken®

CORPORATION

EXECUTIVE OFFICES
P.O. BOX 13331   LOUISVILLE, KENTUCKY 40213
502-459-8600

April 3, 1974

Mr. Lazlo Toth
164 Palm
San Rafael, California

Dear Mr. Toth:

We couldn't agree with you more:

Eagles are for emblems and chicken are for eating.

Sincerely,

John Cox
Director - Public Relations

/re

164 Palm
San Rafael, California
May 8, 1974

The Very Rev. Father John McLauglin S.J.
High Priest of The White House and
Deputy Special Assistant to Our President
The White House
Washington, D.C.

Dear Father McLauglin,

I saw you on T.V. a few days back and now I just
saw an article about you in my newspaper.
Ronald Ziegler used to be my favorite administration
spokesman, then I liked Dean Burch a lot, and then,
whamo - you came on the scene! Talk about sincerity!
And since I'm Catholic (the best) I'm a little part-
ial towards you. Our President sure can use you
now! Too bad you weren't there earlier - then maybe
none of this would have happened!

I'm glad you condoned our President's speech patterns.
I have a friend who works at Motorola and he tells me
all big businessmen talk like that (with a lot of
expletives) and I'll bet the Pope even says a few
cuss words now and then. Am I right? I don't see anything wrong with it as long as you don't take our lord's
name in vain. As much as I love our President, I'd
drop him like a hot potatoe if I heard he was taking
our lord's name in vain! That's serious! Like that
Sister Janice Meade and the rock and roll Our Father.
You and our President should do something about that!
Next thing you know they'll be dancing to the Act of Con-
trition. (My favorite prayer - even more than the Hail
Mary, #3)

Here's a dollar. Please say a low mass for our President. You don't have to put it in the bulletin that it's
for Him, it may embarrass him, just put, "Special Intention, Lazlo Toth". And keep up speaking up for Richard
M. Nixon! He won't forget you when he gets back on his
feet! Someday it might be Cardinal McLauglin! You sure
deserve it!

Gloria! Gloria! Gloria! Pro deo et Patria! Stand by
our flag! Forever!

Do you think it's time yet to start praying to St. Jude
for our President? Many of my friends that I pray with
say "yes" but I think praying to the Saint of Impossible
Causes is extreme and not positive. Who's right?

                              Jesus, Mary and Joseph,

                              Lazlo Toth
                              Lazlo Toth

164 Palm
San Rafael,
California
May 11, 1974

President Richard M. Nixon (the best)
President of the United States
The White House
Washington, D.C.

Dear Mr. President,

I got a letter from Roland Elliott where he
says you liked the song. I knew you would,
I just felt it.
We could put The Star Spangled Banner or
something like that on the other side or we
could put another original. It would be to
our advantage to do another original - most
of the money is going to be in publishing.
I don't have to, but I decided to split it
half and half, fifty-fifty with you. After
all, you did inspire the tune!
I just got done writing another song and I
like it even better than Be True To Your
President! Maybe both will become hits! It's
called Richard Nixon Don't Resign For Me.
(To the tune of Oh Suzanna!)

               Richard Nixon Don't Resign For Me
                              by Lazlo Toth

          The press has been coming down on you
          like buzzards on a dead skunk
          They can't fool the American people
          with leftist literary junk
          Richard Nixon Don't Resign For Me
          You're the best President, that's for sure
          Oh Don't Resign For Me.
                         (repeat three times then
                          start over again.)

If people have something they can sing and
march to it sure helps. That's been true since
the days of Il Duce.

Don't let the press make Watergate your Waterloo!
Fight! Fight! Fight!
Everybody fibs and swears a little. If it wasn't
for a fib or two a lot of big people wouldn't be
where they are today! You know that!

                              Nuts to them!
                              Lazlo Toth
                              Lazlo Toth

THE WHITE HOUSE

WASHINGTON

May 31, 1974

Dear Mr. Toth:

On behalf of the President, I want
to thank you for your thoughtful
message of support. Your friendship
and the unfailing confidence which
you have expressed in the President's
leadership mean a great deal to him
at this time. Please be assured he
will continue to do all that is within
his power to merit the faith you have
placed in him. You may be certain
the President has no intention of
resigning, but rather is determined
to complete the job the American
people elected him to do.

With the President's appreciation
and best wishes,

Sincerely,

Roland L. Elliott
Special Assistant
to the President

Mr. Lazlo Toth
164 Palm
San Rafael, California

Enclosure

164 Palm
San Rafael,
California
May 12, 1974

Boss of the White House Mailroom
The Mailroom
The White House
Washington, D.C.

Dear Boss of the White House Mailroom,

Greetings! I'm sure life in the bins of the most
important mailroom in the world isn't all glamour
and prestigue and I want you to know that here sits
one American who appreciates all you are doing to
keep that little function of yours running smoothly.
The turnover at that place has been fantastic and I
know it must be tough just keeping up with new names.

However, you might try to forward your mail a little
quicker. I wrote to Bob Haldeman on March 6th and
didn't get a letter back from him until May 9th!
And he said the fault was yours! He was being nice
just to say, "it took awhile for the letter to reach
me from the White House", but I could tell, he was
quite upset. Two months! No wonder our President is
having trouble! Get on the ball! Come on! We've
got a country to run here - stop spending all the time
in the cafeteria talking to the secretaries! The
White House is no playground! America is dependent on
you and you are procrastinating! Rome is burning, boss!
Set an example for your men! Move it! What's the
trouble, do you have tired blood?

I hope you get my point.

If our President resigns (he never will) or if, God
forbids, he is impeached and convicted, what happens to
you? I hope you will be able to go with him to Florida.
He'll still be getting a lot of mail. Or, maybe you
could get a job in the mailroom of J. Walter Thompson.
I could ask Bob to get you in there. Or, I could get
you in at Mr. Bubble -- I have a good friend there!
Just call M. Hershey and tell her you're a friend of
mine. Glad to do it for you!

You have one of the jobs in this world that is amall
but big at the same time. If it wasn't important, why
would there be so many mail boxes? Tell them that next
time someone says something to you at one of those fancy
D.C. cocktail parties! Now get back to work! Move it!

> Just helping our President,
>
> *Lazlo Toth*
>
> Lazlo Toth

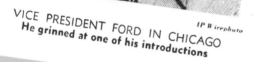

VICE PRESIDENT FORD IN CHICAGO
IP Wirephoto
He grinned at one of his introductions

LSD in Coffee At Ford Speech

Chicago

The hallucinatory drug LSD was found in a coffee urn brewing backstage at a theater where Vice President Gerald Ford spoke last week, authorities said yesterday.

But they said that Ford had no coffee while he was at the theater and that it was not discovered until about nine hours after he had left.

Federal agents said they are investigating. Daniel Hurly of the Secret Service said that he "seriously doubted that anything had been done to injure the vice president but that "we are checking into it."

Ford addressed the National Computer convention last Thursday at the Arie Crown Theater in McCormick Place.

About nine hours after Ford's appearance, six stagehands who drank the coffee became lightheaded and giggly and were hospitalized, police said.

Associated Press

164 Palm
San Rafael, California
May 16, 1974

Vice President Gerald Ford
Vice President of the United States
c/o President Richard M. Nixon (the best)
The White House
Washington, D.C.

Dear Mr. Vice President Ford,

I just read in the paper where someone tried to
put LSD in your coffee in Chicago. Are you okay?
I decided to write as soon as I heard about it.
Are you still on it? Don't try to write back if
you're still on it, your health is more important
than my letter. I just hope there was no damage
to your chomosomes!

I bet the same people did it that tried to put
LSD in the Chicago water system during the 1968
Demo convention. Once they put LSD in Mayor Daley's
ministrone when he was in San Francisco to accept
the St. Francis of Assisi award from Mayor Alioto.
Was he with you when it started to come on? I hope
so, he'd know how to handle it! If it wasn't for
Richard Daley, Hubert and Muriel would be in the
White House today and you would be eating Swiss
Steak at some Moose Hall in Michigan! Daley's hand-
ling of the convention scene got Nixon elected,
you know that! Just because he's a Democrat doesn't
mean he doesn't love our President! He does! He's
as much a freedom loving patriot as you and our
President, that's for sure!

If our President ever decides that this country
no longer deserves him and he wants to just go
fishing and unwind then you would be President!
"President Ford" they will call you! And if that
happens I hope you won't forget Richard J. Daley
when it comes time to name your new V.P. You also
could name Agnew! A lot of people would respect
you for giving him another chance! Or, you could
let people vote. But that wouldn't be right. They
didn't get to vote for you! Why spoil them!

Keep standing up for Richard M. Nixon! He put you
where you are! He ain't heavy, he's your President!

Watch your weight!

NO REPLY !

Lazlo Toth

                                    164 Palm - San Rafael, Calif.
                                    May 17, 1974

Mr. James J. Kilpatrick
c/o The Washington Star (Not the Post, please!)
225 Virginia Avenue SE (South East)
Washington, D.C. (Our Nation's Capitol)

Dear Mr. Kilpatrick,

I just saw you interviewed on the news. You were talking about
how you interviewed our President. You did a great job but I
think you made a BIG mistake when you started talking about his
eyes.
Once I was talking with this Democrat at a party for my friend's
retirement and we started talking about you and Von Hoffman and
your show and he asked me, "Mr. Toth, I bet you don't even know
why they call the program 60 MINUTES." I said,"Of course I do!"
My friend Tuttle, it was his retirement party, said, "It's because the program is one hour long." Everybody there agreed
with Tuttle, and the liberal said, "Do you agree, Mr. Toth?" I
knew where he was going way before he got there! I said, "No,
I do not agree! If the reason the show was called 60 MINUTES
was because it was one hour long, they would have called the
show ONE HOUR instead of 60 MINUTES. The correct answer is because the program is 60 MINUTES long!" The weasel liberal just
smiled. I showed him that you don't have to be born in Moscow
to be in sync with his type of shifty psych! The liberal press
works like this all the time and when you said what you said
about our President's eyes, I said, "Look out, James!"

You said in your interview that when you asked our President a
question that referred to his daughter Julie's Press Conference,
"He closed his eyes and his eyes misted over and he said, "Julie"."
The lefty press is going to jump on you and say, "Mr. Kilpatrick,
how do you know his eyes misted over? You said they were closed!"
They'll bring an ophthalmologist in to testify that a person (you!)
cannot detect if another person's eyes (our President's eyes)
mist over if the person's eyes (our President's eyes) are closed.
They'll make a Federal Case out of it! They'll get you indicted!
You're in trouble! They have a case! You said his eyes were
closed and there is no way you could have seen his eyes mist over
if they were closed!
You could say you meant that his eyes misted over after he opened
them but it would be wrong because you already said his eyes were
closed. But, lucky for you, Toth is here with a way out. You
could say that our President told you that his eyes misted over
while he had them closed!

I helped you out this time but I won't always be able to watch
every word you say. Be careful! The commies have traps set for
all right thinking people! This is war! If things get real bad
I bet our President will let you move in at Camp David with him.
He likes you, too!

Keep standing up for our President! Maybe if those lunatic-do-
nothing Kohouteks in the Congress don't convict him he will make
you his new Press Secretary! You deserve it, that's for sure!

                        What's Right is Right!

                        Lazlo Toth
                        Lazlo Toth

JAMES JACKSON KILPATRICK
WHITE WALNUT HILL
WOODVILLE, VIRGINIA 22749
——
(703) 987-8289

17 June 1974.

Dear Mr. Toth:

Many thanks for your letter, but let me suggest that you say "pfui" for me to your nit-picking friends.

When I am writing for publication, I like to choose my words with some care, but as often as not my purpose is to convey a general impression, not to undertake (as in the case you cited) some sort of opthalmic dissection. Change the "pfui" to "nuts!".

Sincerely,

James J. Kilpatrick.

Mr. Lazlo Toth,
164 Palm,
San Rafael, California.

vs.

164 Palm
San Rafael, California
May 27, 1974

Mr. Colon Stokes
Chairman of the Board
R.J. Reynolds Company
401 North Main Street
Winston-Salem, North Carolina

Dear Mr. Stokes,

I read an interview of you in the Los
Angeles paper and I must say, I was
impressed! I've been a smoker for
years and years and I hate to see the
American tobacco industry take all the
blame for what's happened to this
country in the last twenty years. When
you said, "Smokers are not about to let
the grandstand tactics of the antismoking
forces frighten them into abandoning
their smoking pleasure", I could have
burst out in applause. It sounds just
like something I could have said! Thank
you Jesus!

The first thing they did was make you
put that commie WARNING on every pack
and advertisement and now they're trying
to harass you more. Enough is enough!
If the damn press would lay off the health
news for awhile we could all live in peace
for awhile before we die! After all, we
all have to go! The show must go on! And
you can bet your sweet advanced filter
that another generation of Americans who
love tobacco as much as we do is right
behind us! Tobacco is eternal! Like our
flag!

Stand by our President....like a cigarette
company should!
I'd walk a mile for him!
You can use those. It would be to your
ad-VANTAGE. Get it?

Three packs a day,

Lazlo Toth

Lazlo Toth

RJR

R. J. Reynolds Industries, Inc.
Winston-Salem, N. C. 27102

Colin Stokes
Chairman

June 20, 1974

Mr. Lazlo Toth
165 Palm
San Rafael, California 94901

Dear Mr. Toth:

You were very thoughtful to write such a nice
letter to me after reading an interview relating
to my recent visit to your beautiful state.
(Incidentally, my tardiness in replying is due
to the fact that from California I went on to
Alaska and the Far East before returning to
North Carolina.)

I appreciate your interest in the efforts of our
company and the tobacco industry in combatting
the attacks of the anti-smoking critics. As you
know, statements favorable to the industry are
seldom given the same attention by the media
as are the more sensational charges made by
those who oppose smoking.

It is encouraging to know that you agree with
our stance, and I thank you for taking the time
and trouble to give me your view.

Every good wish.

Sincerely,

Colin Stokes

CS/bw

164 Palm
San Rafael, Calif.
June 5, 1974

Mr. Bebe Rebozo
c/o The White House
Washington, D.C.

Dear Bebe,

I take it you passed on my suggestion about
the "that's for sure" stuff to our President.
Thanks!
I've been reading about all the hoopla the
press is making out of what they're calling
"ethnic slurs". You'd think they never used
one the way they carry on!
As I understand it now, our President denies
he called Sirica a "WOP" and a few lawyers,
"JEW BOYS".
What if he did?
What's wrong with identifiable geographic
nicknames and affectionate religious refer-
ences? Nothing!
But if he called those people those names,
you can bet your $100,000 that the press will
act like it was Pearl Harbor or something.
I suggest you put Ziegler out there in front
of the mikes to say, "Any normal American whose
hearing isn't impaired by marijuana or other
liberal staples can hear that our President
called Judge Sirica a "HOP". A "HOP" in White
House slang is a go-getter." And he can say
that "JEW BOY" means "Julie's boy", that the
President calls men JEW BOYS if his daughter
likes them. A JEW BOY is someone that Julie
likes! Who could get upset if JEW BOY means
someone is liked by that lovely laced daughter
of democracy? Nobody!

I hope you follow me! Lots of luck on this
thing -- I think you can handle it from here.
Fight! Fight! Fight! Stand by our President!

                    Your buddy,

                    Lazlo

                    Lazlo Toth
P.S.
Sometimes people "look like" they have a lot
of money but they really don't. Probably when
you go out with our President you don't let
him pay. Good for you! Here's a dollar I'll
throw in! After all, he's my President, too!

C. G. Rebozo
KEY BISCAYNE BANK BUILDING
KEY BISCAYNE, FLORIDA 33149

July 11, 1974

Mr. Lazlo Toth
164 Palm
San Rafael, California

Dear Mr. Toth:

Thank you very much for your recent note.

It is impossible for me to adequately express my
appreciation for your thoughtfulness.

In times like these, most people, regardless of
their sentiments, don't take the trouble to express
themselves as you did.

Gratefully,

C. G. Rebozo

CGR:nm

164 Palm
San Rafael,
California
June 6, 1974

President
Datsun Car Company (JAPAN)
c/o Nissan Motors
American (Best) Headquarters
18501 S. Figueroa Street
Carson, California

Dear President of Datsun,

Greetings from the United States of America! I
hope my letter reaches you in Japan. If my letter
is anything like your cars, it will reach its des-
tination just fine! How are you?

I was just listening to my radio (American) and I
heard a commercial that said, "Freedom is just another word for Datsun". It was a clever little
tune! (Move over soft drinks!) But when I first
heard it, I have to admit, it made me a little
squeasy (queasy with a smile). But then I thought,
well, that's Freedom of Speech (now also known as
Datsun of Speech) and even our former enemies have
a right to it! After all, you copied everything
else we did!
You Japanese people have done alright! And so have
the Italianos and the Germans! It's the "winners"
of WWII that arn't doing too well! Take a look at
"Great" Britain! Remember the British Empire? Today it's an island! They used to say, "The sun
never sets on the British Empire". Today it sets
at 7:51, tomorrow at 7:52, get it? Translate that
to Japanese and use it! Consider it another helping hand from the U.S.A. - even though nobody gives
us zero! No offense.

You people have done okay because you know how to
play ball, and Capitalism is better off with Datsun
in the boat! You guys are short and can move fast
and mass produce, and even though you can't turn
out beauties like Detroit, you're making great head-
way with those little tunes! Keep it up!

                          Banzai!

                          Lazlo Toth
                          Lazlo Toth

NISSAN MOTOR CORPORATION in U.S.A.

NATIONAL HEADQUARTERS · 18501 SOUTH FIGUEROA ST., CARSON, CALIFORNIA 90248
MAILING ADDRESS: P. O. BOX 191. GARDENA, CALIFORNIA 90247 *phone (213) 532-3111*

June 20, 1974

Mr. Lazlo Toth
164 Palm
San Rafael, Calif.

Dear Mr. Toth:

Your recent letter to our President has been passed along to
me. We greatly appreciate your thoughts regarding our current
advertising program and hope that you are just as favorably
impressed by the new Datsun advertising campaign, "Drive a
Datsun-Help Send a Kid to Y Camp", which will break in the
San Francisco area in approximately one week. During the two
month duration of that campaign, money will be donated in the
name of every person who takes a Datsun test drive at a par-
ticipating dealership. Our target is 250,000 test drives and
if we reach that mark we'll be able to contribute sufficient
funds to the YMCA campership program to send at least 5,000
needy boys and girls to Y camp.

We'd be most pleased if you were in a position to take a
test drive and "Help Send a Kid to Y Camp".

Best wishes,

NISSAN MOTOR CORP. IN U.S.A.

Mayfield Marshall, Jr.
Vice President, Public Relations

MM/jf

164 Palm
San Rafael,
California
June 7, 1974

Dr. Henry A. Kissinger
Secretary of State (U.S.A.)
The White House
Washington, D.C. (if traveling, please forward)

Dear Dr. Secretary,

Congradulations! You did it again! The newspapers are calling you a genius for making the
Arabs and Israelis stop fighting and you certainly deserve it!
However, you should give credit where credit is
due! You shouldn't forget the person who taught
you all you know! The person who made you who
you are today! The person who gave you the opportunity to fly all over the world for free
making peace! Richard M. Nixon! The best President this country has ever known! And I'm
counting Lincoln in there, too! Lincoln looks
good in the history books but times weren't so
complicated then! Afterall, they didn't even
have cars! That's how backwards they were! If
it were only possible to have our President debate him, there would be no contest! Lincoln's
liberal ideas wouldn't stand a chance against
our President's approach to government! If you
were Secretary of State under Lincoln, you'd still
be on the boat on the way there! That proves it!

How's your new wife? I hope you are paying for
her tab when you do all that traveling. The commie press is just watching for stuff like that to
use against our President. Whenever you travel,
get receipts! Or use credit cards -- that way
when you get the bill you can also use it to show
you paid!
I hope your wife is a good traveling companion
and that you don't miss dating. Someone told me
that dating stuff was all public relations and
that our President insisted you go out with all
those Hollywood sex bombs just to make you look
human. Anyway, I'm glad you've got that new
wife (a good cover) so you can concentrate on
helping our President and not have to worry about
wining and dining those starlet kooks and having
to go around looking like you were a sales rep
for Frederick's of Hollywood or something.

You are loved all over the world!
(Just like Coca-Cola!)

Lazlo Toth
Lazlo Toth

DEPARTMENT OF STATE

Washington, D.C. 20520

July 19, 1974

Lazlo Toth
164 Palm
San Rafael, California

Dear Lazlo,

Secretary Kissinger has asked me to reply to your recent
letter. It is heartening to him to receive thoughtful
messages like yours.

You may be sure that you have his deep appreciation for
your support and good wishes.

Sincerely yours,

Carol C. Laise
Assistant Secretary
for Public Affairs

164 Palm
San Rafael,
California
June 7, 1974

Mr. John D. Ehrlichman
Former Chief Advisor on Domestic Affairs
c/o The White House
Washington, D.C. (Our Nations Capitol)

Dear John,

I saw you on the evening news denying you
received payments from a secret legal de-
fense fund. They said our President gave
Bebe Rebozo $400,000 to pay for legal fees
for you and Bob Haldeman. You said it was
all hog wash and that the only place you
were getting money was from common folks
like me and that our President didn't give
you a penny! And then I saw in the paper
where Simon gave a kid a commendation for
bringing in $25 worth of pennies to help
ease the current shortage. What gives?
What is the press trying to pull over our
eyes this time? If Rebozo had the $400,000
plus the $100,000 he got from Hughes, all
together it would be $500,000! Half a mil-
lion dollars in American currency! If it
was in pennies that would certainly account
for the shortage but it's way too much for
a man to carry on his person! Even Rebozo
doesn't have that many pockets! It doesn't
make sense! And the American public will
not fall for it, don't worry!

Here's a buck to help with your expenses.
I know it isn't much, but it will buy you
a sandwich, some fries, and a beverage and
if you go to the right place, you can even
get back change. Know where I mean? Here's
another hint: If you ask for a hamburger
with jelly they'll say,"No! You can only get
jelly with the Egg McMuffin!" Know where I
mean now? Get it?

Keep standing up for our President! He
won't let you down when the going gets
rough! He's not that type!

                    Toth knows you are innocent!

                    Lazlo Toth

August 26, 1974

Mr. Lazlo Toth
164 Palm
San Rafael, California

Dear Mr. Toth:

    I appreciate very much your
taking the time to write me as you
have.

    Letters like yours mean a great
deal to Jeanne and me.

    We are confident that the current
difficulties will fade as we experience
the truth and justice which we know are
at work in this situation.

Yours sincerely,

John D. Ehrlichman

JDE/nd

164 Palm
San Rafael, California
June 10, 1974

Mr. Roland L. Elliott
Special Assistant to the President
The White House
Washington, D.C.

Dear Roland L. Elliott,

Thanks for sending the letter about the President
having no intention of resigning and for the Dent
article <u>The World Can't Do Without President Nixon</u>.
I was hoping you would mention what we should do
with the song. Should I go ahead and make a demo?
It will only cost a couple of hundred bucks. I'd
just go ahead and do it if it was up to me, but I
consider our President my partner in this thing and
if by some one in a million chance the song wouldn't
become a top seller I wouldn't want him complaining
about the cost and that.

I would just write to him directly but every time
I write to him, I get a letter back from you. I
was thinking that maybe if I wrote a letter to you,
I would get a letter back from him. And then I
thought maybe Roland L. Elliott is just a name that
our President uses (like Mark Twain) and that you
are really him! Pretty clever! Keep it up! Fight!
Fight! Fight! Chocolate is good but too much of it
makes you sick. The same goes for freedom of the
press!

I couldn't sleep at all last night (tossing and
turning all night), so I got out my pen and wrote
a new tune. I feel as though it was inspired - like
a miracle. The words just kind of floated in. Just
like geese on the first day of hunting season!

<u>(Our President) Don't Trade Him In</u>
by Lazlo Toth

Country-Folk/Slow dance
To the tune of: <u>You'll Never Walk Alone</u>

Some politicians are like cars,
they were made not to last.
They live their golden hour,
then rust into past.
But Our President is different,
he didn't come off no assembly line.
Otherwise he wouldn't have lasted,
for such a long time.
Don't trade him in, you'll never walk alone.
Don't trade him in, you'll never walk alone.

Lazlo Toth

June 18, 1974

Dear Mr. Toth:

In acknowledging your recent letter, I want
to also express regret that this must be a
disappointing reply. As a matter of long-
standing policy, the President does not
express any opinion on the merits of musi-
cal, literary, or artistic compositions or
take part in introducing or promoting them.
Nevertheless, your courtesy in allowing him
to become familiar with your work is
appreciated.

Sincerely,

Roland L. Elliott
Special Assistant
to the President

Mr. Lazlo Toth
164 Palm
San Rafael, California

164 Palm
San Rafael, California
June 14, 1974
Flag Day!

Mr. Ronald Ziegler
Executive Press Secretary and
Special Assistant to our President
The White House
Washington, D.C.

Dear Mr. Ziegler,

Happy Flag Day! My #4 favorite day! (Armistice
Day, #1. The 4th of July, #2. My birthday, #3.)
Flag Day has always been an important day to me,
so I was especially upset when I picked up this
mornings newspaper, on the 197th anniversary of
our flag and read:
> "At Cairo Airport, the two national
> anthems were played to signify the
> opening of a new era in relations
> between the United States and Egypt.
> The U.S. party looked for an Amer-
> ican flag to face when the military
> band played the Star Spangled Banner
> and there was none in sight."

Whenever I listen to the Star Spangled Banner, as
well as Americans by that Canadian fellow, I like
to keep my eyes on Old Glory the whole time. So,
I know how our President must have felt when he
heard that song and turned to look for a flag to
face and there was none! Don't give me the excuse
that the Arabs were going to bring our flag! Where
would they get it? And even if they said they
could get one, we should have brought one just in
case they forgot it, because evidently they did!
Be prepared! Don't trust foreigners to do an Americans job! I believe in letting bygones be bygones, but I hope that whenever our President
travels in the future you'll bring a flag with you.
I don't mean that you have to carry around a flag
pole - just a small flag that you can carry in
your pocket and hold so our President can face it
when the music starts.

I know that as I write this letter you are still
in the Middle East helping our President make
news, but when you return this letter will be on
your desk waiting for you! So, on behalf of all
the American people, WELCOME BACK! WE MISSED YOU!

Keep helping our President do the job he was elected to do! Keep Richard M. Nixon Number One! Keep
Gerald Ford Number Two!

Lazlo Toth

Lazlo Toth

June 26, 1974

Dear Mr. Toth:

Between the return from the Middle East and
the departure for the Soviet Union, Mr. Ziegler
did have the chance to read your letter of June 14,
although he couldn't answer it personally.

He asked me to write to express his appreciation
for your kind welcome. Certainly it is the strong
patriotism and love of our country as yours which
has helped to keep it so great.

With best wishes,

Sincerely,

Agnes Waldron

Agnes Waldron
Assistant to the
Press Secretary

Mr. Lazlo Toth
164 Palm
San Rafael, California

164 Palm
San Rafael, California
June 17, 1974

Director Mary Brooks
Director of the U.S. Mint
The Treasury Department
15th and Pennsylvania Avenue
Washington, D.C.

Dear Director Brooks,

I saw a picture of you in the paper with Secretary
William Simon. You were giving a commendation to
a little boy for bringing in some pennies to ease
the shortage. It sure was nice of you to help Sec.
Simon, while his head is healing, but I'm puzzled
about the pennies question.

I would like to know how much $500,000 in pennies
would weigh. I would weigh them myself, but I don't
have that many, so I need your help! Would it be
possible for a man (short) to carry that many pennies
on his person? That would be 50 million pennies!
Could 50 million pennies account for the shortage?

Just checking for my own information.

I collect coins!

Lazlo Toth

Lazlo Toth

P.S.
How about a coin for our President!

DEPARTMENT OF THE TREASURY
WASHINGTON, D.C. 20220

OFFICE OF
DIRECTOR OF THE MINT

03 JUL 1974

Mr. Lazlo Toth
164 Palm
San Rafael, California 94902

Dear Mr. Toth:

The Bureau of the Mint and I thank you for your interest
in our coinage.

In answer to your letter of June 17, 1974, the weight of
50 million pennies would be approximately 155,500 kilograms
or about 340,000 pounds.

Sincerely yours,

Roy C. Cahoon
Acting Director of the Mint

Keep Freedom in Your Future With U.S. Savings Bonds

164 Palm
San Rafael, Calif.
June 24, 1974

Rabbi Baruch Korff
National Citizens' Committee for Fairness to the Presidency
1221 Connecticut Avenue NW
Washington, D.C.

Dear Rabbi Korff,

First of all I want to say I think it's wonderful that
you started up a citizens' committee to save our President. It's about time somebody got heard besides the
press! One thing bothers me -- the press gets to say
things against our President for free and we have to
buy space to tell our side! Is that fair? You should
get together with Billy Graham and Father McLaughlin
and say something about that! Equal time for Religion!
That will be a good way of putting it!

I heard that what you're planning next is caravans of
presidential supporters leaving from two dozen cities
in mid-July and finally converging on Capitol Hill July
18th. What an idea! Did J. Walter Thompson come up
with that or did you think of it yourself? It's really
brilliant! Count me in! My car isn't new, but I'll do
anything I can to help my President! Will we be getting
any discounts along the way? (Mariotts?) I'd like to
know because I have to make up my budget. Also, it would
be cheaper for me if I could share gas expenses with
someone. (Male only! If you let men and women drive together, the press will blow it up to look like a Presidential supporters' sex rally! Make a rule!) I would
like to take more than one person, but I don't have the
room. I'll have my Dobermans with me! Does Mariott
allow dogs? Does it cost extra?

Keep up the good work! Here's a small donation to help
pay for the ads. I know the Teamsters Union is giving
you financing, but it looks better if you keep getting
donations from everyday folks, too. After all, who needs
our President more, the Teamsters or the people?

                    Hail to the Chief! I'd
                    drive anywhere for him!

                    Lazlo Toth

                    Lazlo Toth

NATIONAL CITIZENS' COMMITTEE FOR FAIRNESS TO THE PRESIDENCY

NON-PROFIT   INCORPORATED   NON-PARTISAN

WASHINGTON HEADQUARTERS: 1221 CONNECTICUT AVE. N.W., WASHINGTON, D.C. 20036 • 202-347-6597

Dear Friend:

    Your contribution to CARAVAN '74 has been received and is much appreciated.

    In order to make it possible for a maximum number of people to attend, we have done our best to keep the cost down. Accordingly, gifts such as yours are particularly welcome in helping to meet the expenses of this all-important project.

    We are sorry that you cannot be with us in person.

Very sincerely,

Baruch Korff, President

NATIONAL CITIZENS' COMMITTEE FOR FAIRNESS TO THE PRESIDENCY

NON-PROFIT   INCORPORATED   NON-PARTISAN

NATIONAL HEADQUARTERS: 1221 CONNECTICUT AVE. N.W., WASHINGTON, D.C. 20036 • 202-347-6597

General Chairman	President and Chief Executive Officer	Treasurer	Secretary
Mr. Othal Brand	Rabbi Baruch Korff	Mr. Joseph E. Fernandes	Atty. Thomas W. Pearlman

Vice-Chairmen

Mr. Olof V. Anderson   Mr. Lindley Camp   Mr. P. Hoyt Fitch   Maj.Gen. James C. Fry, USA (ret.)   Mr. Jack Kahn
Maj.Gen. Julius Klein, USA (ret.)   Prof. Walter O. Moeller   Mr. Paul B. Shoemaker   Prof. Ernest van den Haag

Dear *Laylo Toth* :

This will acknowledge receipt of the registration form for CARAVAN '74 which you forwarded to us. We look forward to your arrival and shall do all that we can to make your participation in this event a rewarding experience.

Very sincerely yours,

Elizabeth Mudge
Assistant to Rabbi Korff

(over)

Thank you for your support. We do not know, at this time, of any group transportation from the San Rafael area. We would surely be pleased if you were able to come & bring others, too, if possible.

The Shore Inn does allow dogs. There is no extra charge, but owners do have to sign some sort of waiver so the hotel will not be held responsible in case of injury, etc.

164 Palm
San Rafael, California
June 19, 1974

His Most Gracious Majesty
King Faisal
King of Saudi Arabia and
Crown Prince of Petroleum Products
Jidda, Saudi Arabia

Dear King Faisal, your Holiness,

Even though you cut off our oil a few months back, I
never considered it personal, and I always liked you
and your Ulta-Conservative ways!
I remember in 1945 when your Father met Roosevelt on
a boat in the Suez Canal. Your Father took 45 live
sheep with him on the boat. (They wouldn't let him
take his harem on board! Navy rules!) But you don't
have to go to no boat -- the President of the United
States came to you! And a better one than the one
that wouldn't let him bring his harem on board -- the
best since Hoover! Richard M. Nixon! Your friend!
A fellow conservative who knows how to play ball!

I read in TIME magazine (I think you call it TEA-MAY)
that during the farewell ceremonies with our President,
you took an extraordinary step and allied yourself with
our President in his fight against impeachment. You
called on Americans to rally around President Nixon, and
you said that anybody against Nixon is against you!
Bravo! Bravo! Bravo! If you're sitting down when you're
reading this, then stand up! That's how much I think of
you! Go ahead, stand up again! What a King!
We conservatives must stick together and I have an idea
of how you can really help our President fight impeachment!
More than words! It would be wrong, but you could say
that if your friend Nixon is impeached, you will cut off
the oil again. That will stop the commie Demos! You can
make it look unpatriotic for them to impeach him! And
don't think our President will not appreciate the help!
He'll probably give you a state! How about Maine? (You
wouldn't have to live there -- you could always lease it
to some other country!) Think it over! And stay conservative! Not like Morocco!
In the past in Morocco (last year), if a person was caught
stealing, they would cut off the thief's hand in the town
square. Today, they take the thief to the hospital and
do it surgically! They give the thief an anesthetic and
everything! They're making it like a country club! If a
thief knows that his only punishment is a clean, relative-
ly painless amputation, he'll just go ahead and steal things!
You have to be stiff! If people don't suffer a little, they
don't learn! You know that! That's why you cut off our
oil! You showed us that you meant business!
Keep standing up for Richard M. Nixon! He understands you!

NO REPLY! Send me your autograph!

Lazlo Toth

Lazlo Toth

164 Palm
San Rafael, California
July 3, 1974

M. Hershey
Gold Seal Company
10303 Northwest Freeway
Suite 514
Houston, Texas 77018 - ZIPCODE

Dear M,

Hi! I just saw the good news and I must say I am
delighted! I was hoping that you would take my
suggestion and take "KEEP DRY" off the package,
but to go and make a liquid out of it was a real
surprise for me. Thanks!

I knew you would see my point but it was really
clever of you to go ahead and make it and then
just put it out there in the store knowing I would
see it!

How are you feeling? Is your car running okay?
How much is gas there? Get some twenty pound bags
of sugar and keep it in your basement and if you
don't have a basement, put it in your closet. It
will come in handy when the depression hits. I've
just stocked up on bubble bath, too. Guess you can
guess what kind! My favorite - <u>MR. BUBBLE LIQUID</u>!

Stand by our President! I'll take those coupons
now.

Your friend,

Lazlo Toth

Lazlo Toth

NO REPLY !

164 Palm
San Rafael, California
July 10, 1974

Rev. Father John McLaughlin S.J.
Assistant to our President and
High Priest of the White House
The White House
Washington, D.C.

Dear Father,

I've been waiting to hear from you about the
date for the mass. I read in the paper that
the Pope made a new rule that Priests had to
say masses within a reasonable amount of time
after people paid, and I wondered what was
taking you so long. Do you have a lot of masses
to say for him? That's what I was thinking.
Backlog! But then someone told me you were sum-
moned by your Jesuit superiors to Boston for
"prayer and reflection". Then I heard that song
on the radio that says, "PLEASE COME TO BOSTON
FOR THE SUMMER", then it says, "I'M THE NUMBER
ONE FAN OF THE MAN FROM TENNESSEE" - I bet they
changed that from, "I'M THE NUMBER ONE FAN OF
THE PRIEST FROM WASHINGTON, D.C.", am I right?
How does it feel having a song written about
you? Congradulations! You sure got popular
fast! You're another Lee Travino, you are!
Next thing they'll be wanting you to do commercials. Think about it, there's good money in
that! Do you think you could get permission from
your superiors? I'll keep my fingers crossed.

What about the St. Jude thing? I can't hold off
my prayer group forever.

Keep standing up for Richard M. Nixon. He's
going to beat this thing! With your prayers and
connections he can do it! Why don't you suggest
that the Pope comes out with a good word for him?
It wouldn't hurt!

            Jesus, Mary, Joseph and Richard M. Nixon,

                Lazlo Toth

            Lazlo Toth

THE WHITE HOUSE

WASHINGTON

August 27, 1974

Dear Mr. Toth:

It was very thoughtful of you to have written,
and your sincere message of encouragement
is greatly appreciated.

Since it has been my policy not to accept
stipends for Masses while serving at the
White House, I am returning your donation.

Please be assured, nevertheless, that your
intentions will be remembered in my Masses
and prayers.

With every best wish.

Sincerely,

John McLaughlin
Deputy Special Assistant
to the President

Mr. Lazlo Toth
164 Palm
San Rafael, California

Enclosure

164 Palm
San Rafael,
California
July 11, 1974

President
Hershey Chocolate Company
Hershey, Penn.
U.S.A.

Dear Mr. President,

With pain in my fingers I type this letter.
I have enjoyed your candy for years (with and
without nuts) and always thought of you as
the General Motors of the candy world, but I
had a shock, I'll say, this afternoon.

I couldn't believe it when I looked down in
my hand and saw the enclosed deformed M&M.
For as long as I can remember, I never saw
anything but perfect M&M's - what is this
country coming to? It may be just a little
piece of candy - but it means so much more.
It is another little sign that America the
Beautiful is losing status. What if that
pack of M&M's was exported? How would it
look to foreigners? If the Russians saw it,
they'd probably attack! It makes me ashamed
to be an American. Watergate is enough, but
this puts the cap on the bottle. I'm just
glad Hoover isn't alive to see this.

We must stop this type of thing from happening.
"It's just a piece of candy" is a bad attitude
for the leading country in the world to have.
Find out who is responsible for this and fire
them! Make an example! If you don't, a year
from now whole packs will look like they were
made by the Jukes family and not the Hershey's!
Family pride! Keep old glory flying! Oh say
do those perfect M&M's keep coming in the land
of the brave and the home of the free! Play ball!
Stand up for our President!

                    Here's a word that I know
                    you love -- EASTER! One
                    man's bad day is a chocolate
                    company's gain! That's okay,

                    Lazlo Toth

                    Lazlo Toth

encl: 1 (one) deformed M&M.

 **Hershey Foods**

Hershey Foods Corporation
Hershey Chocolate & Confectionery Division
Hershey, Pennsylvania 17033
Phone: (717) 534-4200

July 29, 1974

Mr. Lazlo Toth
164 Palm
San Rafael, California   94901

Dear Mr. Toth:

We regret that one of our HERSHEY-ETS you recently received was imperfect.
Mr. Mohler, our President, has asked me to reply.

Our products are processed and handled by the most modern methods known to
the industry. We subject them to both mechanical and visual inspections and
take special precautions to assure that they leave our plants in perfect
condition. In the case of the improperly molded HERSHEY-ET you received our
efforts at perfection apparently failed.

We appreciate your bringing this matter to our attention, and I want you
to know that our Quality Assurance Staff will intensify its efforts to
maintain perfection in our products.

We are sending you some chocolate which we hope will serve to restore your
faith in our products. If this chocolate is damaged in the mail, please
inform us so we can try again.

                    Very truly yours,

                    (Mrs.) Joan M. Gibble
                    Consumer Information

JMG:baf

164 Palm
San Rafael,
California
July 20, 1974

Mr. Gordon Sinclair
Radio Station CFRB
Toronto,
CANADA

Dear Mr. Sinclair,

I used to have a favorite song and it was
called Birthday Thank You Tommy from Viet
Nam. I used to play it all the time, then
slowly I forgot about it. Then I heard
your song, Americans - and I loved it at
first listen. Talk about spirit! Six months
later and I'm still playing it! If the people
of America could just hear that song all the
time - when they're working, when they're
driving their cars, etc., this country could
run like a clock The American Way!

And do you know what? The Americans reminded
me once more of Birthday Thank You Tommy from
Viet Nam, and now I play both. So, thank you
for bringing me back to Birthday Thank You
Tommy, too.

It's about time we all stood up for America.
Talk about countries.....the best! The other
countries never did help us just like you
said. But you did forget to mention boats.
Most of the boats in the world today are made
with American metals. This is a fact. And they
don't even say thanks!

How about a picture. Come on!

                    An American,

                    Lazlo Toth

                    Lazlo Toth

NO REPLY !

164 Palm
San Rafael, California
July 31, 1974

President Richard M. Nixon (Fighter!)
The White House
Washington, D.C.

Dear President Nixon (Roland),

Things are not looking good.
I just heard one of those commie newsmen say that you
don't have a chance of beating an impeachment vote in
the House and that you're going to have to take it to
the Senate. Everyone is saying that you are through!
They say that you will resign soon! I say all that talk
is Warmed Over Bologna! W.O.B.! They don't know Richard M. Nixon! R.M.N.!

It didn't look good for you in '45 against Voorhis
either! The odds have always been against you - and
everytime (almost) you overcame them! And you will do
it again! Those Republicans who voted against you on
the Judiciary will be sorry! Tomorrow is another day!

Well, here's the good news we've been waiting for. Last
night I had a dream that your face was on Mr. Rushmore!
I have been asking the Lord for a sign and he gave me
one! Hallelujah! Everything is going to be alright!
You were up there plain as day - right between Abe Lincoln and John Mitchell. So, when I awoke, I wrote this:

    <u>Has anybody here seen Mount Rushmore lately?</u>
    (To the tune of: <u>Abraham, Martin and John</u>.)

    Has anybody here seen Mt. Rushmore lately?
    Did you see who's up there?
    It's Richard M. Nixon, the best that's for sure
    Right between Abraham and John.

    Didn't you love the things he gave us?
    How about China? Wasn't that just won-a-der-ful
    for you and me - wait and see
    Pat's gonna be up there, too.

    Has anybody here seen Mt. Rushmore lately?
    Did you see who's up there?
    It's the pride and joy of Yorba Linda, California
    With George, Thomas, Teddy, Abraham and John.

           - Another song by Lazlo Toth/
             Sticking with Richard Nixon
             like gum on a Polack's shoe!

P.S. Fight! Fight! Fight! *Lazlo Toth*

164 Palm
San Rafael, California
August 5, 1974

Mr. Leonard K. Firestone
The tire magnate and President of Nixon Foundation
c/o Firestone Rubber Company
Akron, Ohio

Dear Mr. Firestone,

I think it's wonderful that you're collecting
for the Nixon library. It's going to be some
place! It could be another Ripley's!

I would like to make my dollar go towards
bullet proof glass. (To protect the librarians!)
But if you already have enough for the glass
for the windows, buy Hoover - What A Man by
Patrick Reynolds. (My #5 favorite book.)

Keep sticking up for Richard M. Nixon! He
will beat this thing! When all the facts are
in, everything will be okay. All the people who
are jumping off the boat now will someday want
back on, and we will say, "sorry chum, no room."
Richard M. Nixon will rise again!

Let me know if you already have a place chosen
for the Nixon library. I have a suggestion of
where you should put it.

                    Richard M. Nixon still has
                    good treads and a lot of
                    wear left in him! You
                    understand that! That's
                    your language!

                    Lazlo Toth

                    Lazlo Toth

P.S. I haven't seen your blimp around lately.
      Still got it?

164 Palm
San Rafael, California
August 6, 1974

President Richard M. Nixon
The White House
Washington, D.C.

Dear President Nixon (Roland),

The water is getting deeper.
Even the so called "conservative" Republican members
of the Judiciary Committee are saying you should resign and that they will vote for impeachment.
And just now Rabbi Korff said he thinks you will resign. POPPYCOCK! Korff and Wiggins and Sandman and
the rest will be sorry when you beat this thing! And
make no bones about it, Richard M. Nixon, Sustainer
Supreme, will sustain! That's for sure!

I wrote to Korff about driving to D.C. to support
you and he didn't write back until the day I was
suppose to be there (July 18th) and he said, "Sorry
you cannot be with us in person." I could have been
there if he would have answered my letter on time!
And the following day I received a letter from his
secretary saying they would be pleased if I came and
would I "bring others". The letter was mailed from
D.C. on the day we were suppose to be there (18th)!

It seems that once again you have picked the wrong
man for an important job! Fire him! Let a man named
Toth take over that Committee! He would strighten
the situation out! I could be there in 8 hours if
you gave me the go ahead. This Watergate thing is
nothing! It's just crisis number seven! You're not
through! You've got lots of crises still in front
of you! You know that!
If you would have listened to me in March and resigned
in April or May you could have kept a nice 30% following and right now you would be down in Florida working
on you '76 ad campaign. But that's water over the damn
gate. Get it? (You can use that.)

"When the going get tough, the toughs get going."
- Pat O'Brian

Fight! Fight! Fight!

NO REPLY !

Hang in there!
This is nothing!

Lazlo Toth
Lazlo Toth

Do you know:

The honorable Richard M. Nixon is the President of our nation who DID end our active participation in the war in Vietnam: who succeeded in returning 550,000 AMERICAN TROOPS and POW's to their homeland: who led the United States to victories in the SPACE PROGRAM: who established

detente with RUSSIA and CHINA: who ended rioting and burning by students in our colleges and subversive elements in our cities.

It is your civil right to be protected by your president from subversives who may sell vital information to our enemies. President Nixon is fulfilling that obligation.

Fellow American
Thanks for your support of this great President

The response to this ad has been wonderful. 97% of the replies are in agreement with our statements. Many call President Nixon our greatest President and would vote for him again. Grass root citizens are calling for an end to the impeachment process and are fed up with Watergate.

The ad has run in leading newspapers in Philadelphia, Detroit, Baltimore, Washington, Chicago, Cleveland, Cincinnati, St. Louis, Boston, Atlanta, Pittsburgh, Richmond, New Jersey and many other cities. The reaction from the real Americans has been uniform. They are with us all the way.

WAS IMPEACHMENT MENTIONED:
AFTER PEARL HARBOR—THE RESULT OF PRESIDENT ROOSEVELT'S SUBORDINATES CARELESSNESS?
AFTER THE BAY OF PIGS INVASION—PRESIDENT KENNEDY'S FIASCO?
AFTER THE TONKIN GULF INCIDENT—The mistake that caused President Johnson to escalate the war in North Vietnam? Do you believe as we do that Watergate is a political issue, blown up completely out of proportion?

DON'T QUIT, MR. NIXON!

Consider this my vote of confidence in your ability, Mr. President, to lead America to Peace and Security. I am joining the millions of people in America who support you.

Name: *LAzlo Toth* Address: *164 PALM*

City, State, Zip: *SAN RAfAel , CALIFORNIA   yes*

(This vote of confidence will be delivered to the President in Washington)

Send today to Committee to Support the President, C.H. Daly, Jr., Chairman, P.O. Box 243, Ridgefield N.J. 07657. If you wish to make a small contribution to help pay for more ads and support, enclose a check payable to Committee to Support the President.

164 Palm
San Rafael, California
August 8, 1974

Citizen/President Richard M. Nixon
Casa Pacifica (The Pacific House)
(Formerly Western White House)
San Clemente, California

Dear President Nixon (Roland),

With my hanky in my hand I write this letter.
I just got finished watching your resignation speech on
T.V. (television). I just cannot believe it! I'm going
to take a bubble bath. I've had it!

                                    August 9, 1974

I hope you're feeling better today. Those suds help, don't
they? I got kicked off a bowling team once so I know what
you're going through. I just decided to forget about the
whole thing instead of getting mad and now (19 years later)
most of them are dead and I'm still bowling. So, you see,
you never know. Twenty years from now you may still be collecting your $163,000 per year plus office space, and all
those do good guys will be planting crops in their front
yards and trying to stretch their social security pittance.

It was smart quitting while you could still get your benefits.
You're entitled to them! Just because you lost your political
base doesn't mean you should lose your pension! Everybody else
can collect from the government, why not you? Just take it
easy. Plant a garden. Set up a croquet course. You've got
it made! You've got the life of a real Don Corleone, you do!

Last night, towards the end of my bath, I wrote this song
for you (my last):
                    Try to Remember to Forget It.
                              by Lazlo Toth
        To the tune of: The Party's Over.

        What good is the bird seed after the bird is gone?
        How good can new days be if old memories linger on?
        It would be wrong to dwell on it, for away it will not go
        (Chorus: That's for sure.)
        Why don't you just try to remember to forget it.

Like you said in your speech, "this is not good-bye, tnis is
au revoir, till we meet again in French".

                    Au Revoir President Nixon!
                    Lazlo Toth says Au Revoir!

                    Lazlo Toth
                    Lazlo Toth

164 Palm
San Rafael,
California
August 9, 1974

President Gerald R. Ford (the best)
The White House
Washington, D.C.

Dear President Ford,

Fight! Fight! Fight!

I'm with ya!

Sincerely,

Lazlo Toth

Lazlo Toth

Thank you for your very kind and thoughtful message of congratulations. It is encouraging to have the goodwill and support of the American people. Working together, I know we can go forward in peace with other nations and in progress here at home.

Gerald R. Ford

2039 High Tower
L.A., California
90068
September 13, 1974

Mr. Philip W. Buchen
Counsel to the President
The White House
Washington, D.C.

Dear Mr. Buchen,

Congradulations on being promoted to the cabinet!
I read that you assembled the legal data on which
President Ford based his decision to pardon President Nixon. Is that what got you promoted so fast
or was it the fact that you and our new President
are old friends? Regardless, you sure deserved it!

Thanks for helping President Nixon! History will
some day judge President Ford's decision to pardon
him a very kind move in the true Christian spirit
under which our Nation was founded.
But don't go pardoning the draft dodgers! Just because they thought the war was wrong shouldn't make
it possible for them to get off scot free like President Nixon! After all, they are not the President!
They must pay for their wrong! What's right is right!

When you were law partners back in Grand Rapids with
our new President did you ever think he would become
President? Yes? No? Please answer.

A Ford Man!

Lazlo Toth

Lazlo Toth

October 10, 1974

Dear Mr. Toth:

Thank you very much for your kind and warm letter
of September thirteenth. It was good of you to
write and express your congratulations on my
appointment.

This is indeed the most difficult but also the
most fascinating assignment I have ever had. My
only aim is to serve the country and the President
to the best of my abilities.

In answer to your question, I must of course write
that I did not think that the man with whom I
began the practice of law would become President
of the United States.

Your letter was truly appreciated.

Warmest regards.

Most sincerely yours,

Philip W. Buchen
Counsel to the President

Mr. Lazlo Toth
2039 High Tower
Los Angeles, California 90068

2039 High Tower
Los Angeles,
California
Sept. 20, 1974

Mr. Howard B. Johnson
President
Howard Johnson Restaurants
P.O. Box 345
Braintree, Massachusetts

Dear Mr. Johnson,

I've been going to your restaurants so long
I feel I can call you Howard. I used to date
a wonderful woman who worked at one of your
places. I was impressed by her cause she knew
all the 28 flavors and she taught them to me.
A couple months ago I ran into her at the Mall
and I said, "How about naming me the 28 flavors",
but she said she forgot them. But Toth remembered them and I said them to her right there
at the Disco check out.

Even though we stopped dating (religious dif-
ferences) I still go to your restaurants. On
your breakfast menu you say, "TWO EGGS, ANY
STYLE". When I told the waitress, "Scrambled
and poached" she said I had to have them both
done the same style. It doesn't say that on
the menu! It says, "TWO EGGS, ANY STYLE", and
that's all! Check it yourself! Paula used to
make one poached and one scrambled for me and I
don't see why the rest can't! What's happening
to this country! Why are all these young people
so lazy? ANY STYLE means ANY STYLE, you know
that! Don't let this happen!

Also, I have a word to say about lettuce. I see
you are still using it under jello and peaches
and things like that. Lettuce is not Christmas
lights! The days of decorating with food are
over! Get wise! If you think lettuce is such a
great decoration, I suggest you paint a drawing
of lettuce on your plates. Or, instead of doing
that, why don't you just draw a picture of a
plate with a picture of lettuce on it right on
the table. This way you can just hose down the
table instead of washing dishes.

Green and Orange is number two
only to Red, White and Blue!!!

Lazlo Toth

Sunday, September 29, 1974

President Gerald Ford
The White House
Washington, D.C.

Dear President Ford,

Yesterday, in your closing remarks before the National Summit
Conference on Inflation, you asked Americans to make a list of
10 Ways to Save Energy and Fight Inflation. You asked that lists
be exchanged among friends and neighbors as well as sent to you.
Tomorrow morning by 7 A.M. (morning) my suggestions will be in
the mail - on their way to all my friends.
Mr. President, here is your copy!
  1. Walk! No one drives unless going more than 5 miles!
     (Example: If you live 3 miles from work (6 round trip),
     drive a half mile - park car - walk rest of way to
     work, then after work walk to car then drive home.)
  2. Go to sleep - 8 o'clock. Late enough!
     (Save lights, wear on clothes, etc.)
  3. Refrigerator Laws:
        Phase 1: Only open three times a day.
        Phase 2: Only open twice a day.
  4. No Heat Above 62 Degrees! (Rest homes, 63.)
  5. Use Hankies, not Kleenex! (You can't wash Kleenex!)
  6. Never toast only one piece of bread because both sides
     of the toaster get hot. If you only eat one piece of
     toast in the morning like me, make two and eat one the
     next day!
  7. Don't flush after every time! Every other time!
     Savings: 50%!
  8. Pull all plugs out of sockets when not in use! (Lamps,
     T.V. (television), toaster, etc.) Prevents electricity
     from leaking into appliances.
  9. Only UP elevators below the 12th floor of buildings!
 10. Start cars in Neutral instead of Park! Save 1/4 of a
     gallon on a full tank! (Tested myself.)

Toth Extras! If things get really bad. (Depression with Honor.)

  1. The Toilet Cloth. See #5 above. (You can't wash toilet paper!)
  2. One Glass of Water Less on Even Numbered Days.
     One Glass of Water More on Odd Numbered Days.
     If every American followed this plan, a heart beat type
     rhythm would immediately develop throughout the country's
     water and sewage systems. This new force could then be
     used to push ships situated in front of the St. Lawrence
     Seaway out to sea and help conserve fuel!
     Savings: 18%

Together we can beat this thing and get this great Nation back
on the roads to the restaurants! Fight! Fight! Fight!

                         Pro Patria Et Deo!

                         Lazlo Toth
                         Lazlo Toth

THE WHITE HOUSE

WASHINGTON

November 5, 1974

Dear Mr. Toth:

Your unhesitating response to my request
for suggestions to stop inflation and
save energy is greatly appreciated. With
the help of ideas from families and individuals across the land our country can
overcome this serious problem. This is
a difficult time for all of us. Victory
is assured, however, by the will and
spirit of Americans to win.

I am enclosing your WIN buttons to show
that you were one of the earliest Inflation
Fighters to enlist. Thank you again and
keep it up.

Sincerely,

Gerald R. Ford

Mr. Lazlo Toth
2039 High Tower
Los Angeles, California   90068

Public Transportation Ideas
ARCO - Box 30169
Los Angeles, California

THE MALLMOBILE

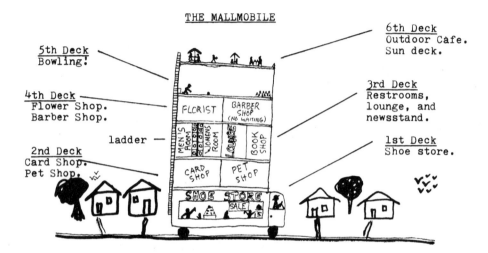

5th Deck
Bowling!

4th Deck
Flower Shop.
Barber Shop.

ladder

2nd Deck
Card Shop.
Pet Shop.

6th Deck
Outdoor Cafe.
Sun deck.

3rd Deck
Restrooms,
lounge, and
newsstand.

1st Deck
Shoe store.

Dear ARCO,

I got this idea from seeing a double decker bus
in a foreign country.
I thought to myself, "It's smart to have two
decks instead of having two buses."
Then I thought, "Instead of people getting into
buses and going shopping, why not bring the
shops to them!"

My MallMobile can go to different neighborhoods
on different days, just like the Milk Man and
Dry Cleaners! This idea helps save a lot of gasoline plus it saves people time because they don't
have to go far - only to the street!

I give this idea free to ARCO (Atlantic Richfield
Company) because of all the things they have given
to us - glasses, windshield scrapers, etc.

We will beat this inflation!

Lazlo Toth

Lazlo Toth

One Idea Ahead of Its Time

Never tell people *how* to do things. Tell
them *what* to do and they will surprise you
with their ingenuity.
  —Gen. George S. Patton

Atlantic Richfield Company, on behalf of its employees, shareholders
and everyone in America who depends on public transportation, salutes

Lazlo Toth

whose Idea Ahead of Its Time can represent one of the important
steps we must take on the way to a better quality of life for all
Americans. This idea, along with many others generated by
thoughtful people throughout the Nation, will help awaken public
opinion to the need for adequate public transportation in America.
We thank you.

T F Bradshaw

Thornton F. Bradshaw
President
Atlantic Richfield Company

September, 1974

2039 High Tower
Los Angeles, California
USA
October 26, 1974

The Right Honorable Pierre Trudeau
Prime Minister of Canada
Ottawa, Canada

Dear Sir:

On behalf of our former President and all the
American people, I would like to take this
opportunity to apologize for what the Press
said our former President called you. (dirty
word)

The Press has been picking on President Nixon
for more than two years, and they would love
to see a war between our countries because
all they care about is selling newspapers and
a war would do it, that's for sure!

Keep serving your country and don't let this
thing come between us! (That's just what
they want!)

                          The USA and Canada!
                          Both countries in
                          North America!
                          Keep it up!

                          Lazlo Toth

                          Lazlo Toth

 Office of The Cabinet du
Prime Minister Premier Ministre

November 18, 1974.

Mr. Lazlo Toth,
2039 High Tower,
Los Angeles, California,
U. S. A.

Dear Mr. Toth:

On the Prime Minister's behalf, may
I thank you for your October 26 letter,
following a recent "Watergate" reference to
the Prime Minister.

Your thoughtful comments are very
much appreciate.

With all good wishes.

Yours sincerely,

Patricia Forbes

(Mrs.) Patricia Forbes,
Correspondence Assistant.

WIN

Dear President Ford:

I enlist as an Inflation Fighter and Energy Saver for the duration. I will do the very best I can for America.

(Please Print.)

Name LAZLO TOTH Date DEC. 10 '74

Address 2039 HIGH TOWER

City LOS ANGELES State CALIFORNIA Zip Code 90068

VOLUNTEERS—Enlistment form for "inflation fighters" can be mailed to the WIN Coordinating Office, Washington, D.C. 20500.
UPI Wirephoto

THE WHITE HOUSE
WASHINGTON

My Fellow Consumer:

Here is a check list to help you be an Inflation Fighter. The following tips can save you and your family money. Please join me and be a part of the team to stop inflation today. Remember, to have a strong, healthy economy we must Whip Inflation Now.

Sincerely,

Virginia Knauer

Virginia H. Knauer
Special Assistant to the President
for Consumer Affairs

Your checklist to WIN:

1. Balance your family budget and expect your government officials to do the same.
2. Use credit wisely.
3. Save as much as you can and watch your money grow.
4. Teach thrift — be an example for others in spending and saving habits and in energy conservation.
5. Travel wisely — use public transportation and car pools whenever possible. Try bike riding — it's fun and good exercise.
✓ 6. Shop wisely, look for bargains and buy the lower cost items and brag about the fact you are a bargain hunter.
7. Waste as little as possible.
8. Join programs for recycling and the re-use of scrap materials.
9. Work with others to eliminate outmoded government regulations that keep costs of goods and services high.
10. Guard your health.

GPO 882-363

December 10, 1974

President Gerald Ford
The White House
Washington, D.C.

Dear President Ford,

I read the cover story on you in <u>Newsweek</u>.
I hope the press isn't going to start picking on you,
too. Next time you have a press conference, go out
there and say:

<u>PRESIDENT</u>: I want you all to know you
can stop worrying that a
depression is coming.
(PAUSE FOR TWO SECONDS)
Because it's here!

<u>PRESS</u>: LAUGHTER AND APPLAUSE

You've got to kid with them more! That's why they
liked Kennedy so much!

Thanks for sending the <u>WIN</u> buttons. But I think that
if we want to <u>W</u>hip <u>I</u>nflation <u>N</u>ow, we've got to do it <u>N</u>.
It took one month for me to get them! I hope it isn't
because some button maker told you it took that long to
print up a few buttons. They sure got them out fast
enough when they had doves on them!
But, more important than buttons, I think we should -
<u>GET RID OF ALL THE GREEN "GO" LIGHTS!</u> Who needs them!
They may be prettier than having just RED, YELLOW, and
NOTHING, but they're bad economics!
I explain: When people see the YELLOW, they will be
cautioned that RED is coming up. They stop for RED,
just like normal, but instead of changing to GREEN (GO),
it just goes OFF. Then, after it's OFF (no light) for
awhile, it changes to YELLOW and then RED. Get it? I
hope you're following me. This is important! There are
hundreds of Stop Lights across this Nation, Mr. President, and every one of them is wasting precious elect-
ricity as well as GREEN light bulbs.

I was telling my friend, George Tuttle, about me sending
you some suggestions to <u>Help Fight Inflation and Save</u>
<u>Energy</u>, and he said that if I really wanted to help fight
inflation and save energy, I would stop my correspondence.
He says my sending letters to people is inflationary. I
got mad and said he was wrong, but later, when I was alone
in my favorite room, I started thinking about it and I
knew he was right. Until the economic situation changes,
<u>I am stopping my correspondence. From now on, I will only</u>
<u>write to people when it is important!</u>

Fight! Fight! Fight!

Lazlo

Lazlo Toth

2039 High Tower
Los Angeles, California
90068 - ZIP CODE
May 24, 1975

Mr. Nguyen Cao Ky
Former South Vietnamese Premier
c/o Food for the Hungry, Inc.
Auburn, California

Dear Premier Ky,

Welcome to California! I was glad to hear you got
out of Camp Pendleton so quick. I guess it was because you have a lot of pull - good for you! There's
no reason why you should waste your time around some
camp!

I hope you and the other former cabinet ministers
will be happy in Auburn. I once stopped at a
McDonald's up there and had a Big Mac and I ate it
in my car as I was driving around. It was quite a
treat - good food plus good scenery - you can't beat
that! Enclosed find one dollar American so you can
have your first Big Mac on me!

Now, let me get to the meat of this letter. I have
always been a strong supporter of yours and think
that if that Thiu guy never became President, and you
were still in charge, we would still have Liberty in
Vietnam! I always liked the way you looked, too!
Kind of like an Oriental Clark Gable! And I'm sure
you'll make it Big in this country, too!

                    Your pal,

                    Lazlo Toth

                    Lazlo Toth

October 15, 1975

Mr. Lazlo Toth
2039 High Tower
Los Angeles, Cal. 90068

Dear Mr. Toth:

Thank you very much for your letter. I apologize for the
delay in answering, but we have been busy finding a place
to settle. We have decided to stay in the Washington area
for the time being as I feel that I can be more effective
here in helping the Vietnamese.

I am writing this note to express my gratitude for your
kind words and good wishes. Also, I would like very much
to thank you for the dollar you sent so that I could get
a hamburger at MacDonalds.

I would like to report to you that a National Center for
Vietnamese Resettlement has been formed in Washington
to assist in the long term needs of the refugees. I know
that we can count on your support of the Center.

Your feelings toward the refugees from Vietnam are heart-
warming and constitute a great source of encouragement to
me. For this and your other kindnesses, I send you my
grateful thanks. Best personal wishes to you.

Yours sincerely,

Nguyen Cao Ky

2282 N. Beachwood
Los Angeles, California
October 23, 1975

President Richard M. Nixon
Casa Pacifica
San Clemente, California

Dear President Nixon (Roland),

I saw your picture on the cover of Newsweek and
saw the pictures of you playing golf with the
Teamsters. You look great!

And I'm happy to hear that you plan on getting
back into public life and making yourself a
"public presence". Bravo! Don't keep the people
waiting any longer! Jump in! We need you!

As a former President of this Nation, we deserve
to have your advice and need it NOW!

                              Your supporter for life,

                              Lazlo Toth

                              Lazlo Toth

P.S.   I see you have a new dog - Vicki.
       What happened to King Timahoe?

RICHARD NIXON

LA CASA PACIFICA
SAN CLEMENTE, CALIFORNIA

November 7, 1975

Dear Mr. Toth:

A friendly letter in the mail bag is
always most welcome, and that certainly
was the case with yours of October 23rd.

It was thoughtful of you to take the time
to write as you did, and I wanted you to
know of my appreciation.

With best wishes,

Sincerely,

Richard Nixon

Mr. Lazlo Toth
2282 North Beachwood Drive
Los Angeles, California 90068

P.S. King Timahoe is with us and in the best of
health; Vicki has been in the family since
1962 and is amazingly active and well for
her years.

2282 N. Beachwood
Los Angeles, California
March 2, 1976

President Richard M. Nixon
La Casa Pacifica
San Clemente, California

Dear President Nixon (Roland),

Welcome back! You were <u>great</u>! You can't imagine
how it made me feel to see you in the limelight
once again. The American people need you!

Your China trip was a great achievement for the U.S.
and you have every right to help keep the ball
rolling. President Ford and the others are just
jealous that they aren't leading the way! Don't let
them bully you into taking a back seat - we need
<u>you</u>. True leadership is hard to find! I only wish
you could run for President again!

                        Your supporter for life,

                        Lazlo Toth

                        Lazlo Toth

RICHARD NIXON

April 2, 1976

Dear Mr. Toth:

You were most thoughtful to write us
about our recent trip to China.

Mrs. Nixon and I are indeed grateful
for the friendship and understanding
which the kind comments you included
so warmly convey.

We join in sending our appreciation
and very best wishes to you.

Sincerely,

Richard Nixon

Mr. Lazlo Toth
2282 North Beachwood Drive
Los Angeles, California 90068

VOTE
IN THE PRIMARY
for
Gerald R. Ford

MAN OF PROVEN HONESTY

"My first objective is to have sound economic growth without inflation."

quote

Gerald R. Ford

and

He has . . .

RESULTS

Quote from N.Y. Times, April 25, '76

"Two of the economy's vital signs, the gross national product and the rates of inflation have provided additional and substantial evidence that the United States recovery from the recession is proceeding steadily and with less inflation ... President Ford can reasonably expect that the continuing improvement his Administration forecast last year will aid his campaign for the Republican nomination."

MR. PRESIDENT
said in his
State of the Union

"We can achieve a balanced budget by 1979 if we have the courage and the wisdom to continue to reduce the growth of federal spending. The budget I am submitting cuts this rate of growth in half."

Yet . . .
NOT AT THE EXPENSE
of **YOU!**

WHAT RONALD REAGAN
did as Governor
of California

He more than doubled the spending. From 4.6 billion in 1967 to 10.2 billion in 1973. He stated, "I felt taxes were already a burden." So what did he do? He increased California taxes over 2 billion dollars. As James Reston wrote: "Reagan is not looking for facts but reaching for votes ... the funniest thing that has heppened so far is the emergence of Ronald Reagan as an expert on foreign and military policy ... it's the best miscast part he ever had, but it's more theater than politics."

DO VOTE IN THE PRIMARY, TUES., JUNE 8

Paid by Mike and Mary Ann Keeler, Grand Rapids, Michigan

MEET
JIMMY CARTER

AT
THE FORUM
ON ELECTION EVE
MONDAY, JUNE 7
8 P.M.

LIVE ENTERTAINMENT
FREE ADMISSION

MANCHESTER BLVD. & PRAIRIE AVENUE IN INGLEWOOD
(Off the San Diego Freeway)

2282 N. Beachwood
Los Angeles, California
90068 - ZIP CODE
July 8, 1976

President Gerald Ford
The White House
Washington, D.C.

Dear President Ford,

Just a short note to congradulate you on doing such
a fine job during the Bycentenial. Seeing you in
New York with all those big boats sent chills up and
down my spine!

Some folks I heard talking at the hardware store said
you probably would hit your head on one of those foreign boat booms, but you were as agile as Fred Astaire,
and everybody was impressed - even Democrats! But,
just a word about your bumping your head: It doesn't
bother me when you hit your head getting on airplanes,
against doors, etc., but it bothers me when you always
say "it doesn't hurt". It doesn't? This can give
people the impression that something is the matter with
your nerve endings! Next time you bump your head, say
"it hurts a little". This will make you seem more normal.

And, speaking of not being human, the Queen of England
had some nerve complaining about the choice of songs
for her first dance with you following the wonderful
dinner you gave in her honor. <u>The Lady Is A Tramp</u> is a
fine American tune, she shouldn't have taken it so personal! We should be able to play whatever song we want!
After all, it's our Bycentenial!
She's probably just mad because they lost the war. Too
bad! The way her country has been going, she should be
happy she got a free meal. What nerve! Nuts to her!

Keep doing a good job, my President! And don't worry
about Reagan. I liked him in those Vitalis ads he used
to do, and I liked him in Death Valley Days, but for
President, I like you! Stand by our flag!

                    Bycentenially yours,

                    Lazlo Toth

                    Lazlo Toth

THE WHITE HOUSE

WASHINGTON

July 26, 1976

Dear Mr. Toth:

I appreciated your fine letter.

You will find enclosed a personally
autographed copy of my series of
speeches given during the celebration
of our Bicentennial.

Sincerely,

Jerry Ford

Mr. Lazlo Toth
2282 North Beachwood
Los Angeles, California   90068

1776 — 1976

UNITED STATES BICENTENNIAL

2282 N. Beachwood
Los Angeles, California
USA 90068 - ZIP CODE
July 10, 1976

Her Majesty, The Queen (Gracious)
Buckingham Palace
London, England

Dear Madam _____,

It sure was nice of you to come over here to America to
forgive us and help us celebrate the Bycentenial.

I saw you on T.V. (television) at the dinner President
Ford threw for you and you looked beautiful with that
terrific crown on your head. It reminded me of another
century! You don't have to answer this if you don't
want to - How much is it worth? I was just wondering.

I heard that you were more than a little put off by the
choice of songs President Ford had played at the dinner.
The Lady Is A Tramp is an American classic and you should-
n't have taken it to mean that the song was in any way
referring to you. They probably would have written a
special tune just for you but nobody knows your last name.
We just call you "Queen Elizabeth" over here. "Queen
Elizabeth" who? Let me know your last name and I'll get
working on a proper tune especially for you. It will be
like Won't You Come Home Bill Bailey - so I need to know
your whole name. They wouldn't have written Won't You Come
Home Bill - "Bill Who?", they would have asked. I know when
people say "Queen Elizabeth" they usually think it's you,
but I want to make it perfectly clear. (Don't take any
chances!)

In the meantime, I've written this little tune to try to
make you feel better. It could become your theme song -
better than the one you've got now - too old fashioned!

                    The Lady Is A Queen
                        by Lazlo Toth

She likes America even when it's cold and it's damp,
She's real classy, that's why she's on all the stamps,
She eats all they give her but she always stays lean -
That's why the lady is a Queen. /
The pound may be falling but her nose (it) remains high,
It's like she's from the house of wax except she's alive,
She's really something royal, if she was a he she'd be a King -
That's why the lady is a Queen. /.

                    Come back any time!
                    The English language made
                    this letter possible - where
                    would America be without it?
                    Keep it up!

                    Lazlo Toth
                    Lazlo Toth

P.S. Please send me
     your picture.

BALMORAL CASTLE

21st September, 1976

Dear Mr. Toth,

    I am commanded by The Queen to thank you
for your letter, and to tell you how much
Her Majesty enjoyed her visit to America.

    You have asked for a photograph of The Queen,
but I have to explain to you that, owing to
Her Majesty's rules in these matters, it is not
possible for The Queen to send her photograph to
anyone whom she does not already know personally.
This I feel sure you will understand when I tell
you of the many similar requests that Her Majesty
receives.

    For your information The Queen has no surname,
but belongs to the House of Windsor, of which she
is the Head.

              Yours sincerely,

              Susan Hussey

            Lady-in-Waiting

Mr. L. Toth,
  2282 N. Beachwood,
   Los Angeles,
    California, 90068,
     U.S.A.

2282 N. Beachwood
Los Angeles, California
August 4, 1976

President Gerald Ford
The White House
Washington, D.C.

MEMO TO PRESIDENT FORD FROM LAZLO TOTH

I think it's wonderful that you have asked delegates to
suggest names for you to pick from to choose your new V.P.

I am not a delegate, but I have some suggestions for you.

Since I was a Vice President of a lot of organizations myself,
I have experience and that should be a factor in your choice.
I know you probably would want someone who has held elective
office and I have that - Knights of Columbus!
And something to consider is that I have the same amount of
letters in my last name as you - four! It looks good on buttons!
I know I have a long shot of being chosen in Kansas City, but it
would be good for you to pick someone who doesn't have a Washington background. I've never even been there! Probably none
of the other candidates could claim that! Some others may claim
they've never been there, but can they prove it? This is something that should be checked on! Don't leave it to subordinates!
Look what happened to our former President when he asked Ziegler
to bring the flag to Egypt - disaster! Our President didn't
know which way to turn! I will consider it my duty to take care
of things like that!

Other suggestions:

     Schweiker - Since you're going to beat Reagan (probably),
                 it might be a good idea to appease those Reagan
                 backers by picking his choice for V.P.
     Richard Daley - I know he's a Democrat, but with him on the
                 ticket you would pick up a lot of Catholic voters
                 who are afraid of Carter - plus you would win
                 Illinois. That's a big state! Also, picking
                 Daley will help you with people who will be mad
                 at you if you don't choose Connally - cause
                 Daley has been accused of a lot of shady things,
                 too!
     Maureen Dean - This will get all those militant women in
                 your corner cause they will be delighted you had
                 the guts to pick a woman. Also, Carter won't be
                 able to pick on you for pardoning President Nixon
                 if you pick the wife of the man who started the
                 whole thing as your running mate. Plus, her name
                 also has four letters and she's got experience.

          Onward to Kansas City!   Lazlo Toth
          Good luck!

August 16, 1976

Dear Mr. Toth:

President Ford has asked me to thank you
for your letter and for your thoughtfulness in writing. Your suggestions with
respect to the 1976 Republican Vice
Presidential nominee are appreciated.

The President has not made his decision.
He hopes to be in a position at the Convention to recommend to the delegates
that individual best qualified to be
Vice President and to join with him in
leading our Party to victory in November.

Again, thank you for your interest and
best wishes.

          Sincerely,

          Roland L. Elliott
          Director of Correspondence

Mr. Lazlo Toth
2282 North Beachwood
Los Angeles, California 90068

DEAR LAZLO,

THANK YOU AND PRAISE THE LORD FOR YOUR RESPONSE TO
HELP CLEAN UP TELEVISION. PLEASE PRAY THAT GOD
WILL USE REVIVAL FIRES AND CHRISTIANS LIKE YOU TO
MAKE TELEVISION PROGRAMS FIT TO WATCH.

GOD BLESS YOU.

**I'm holding this beautiful Bicentennial "Wake Up America" plate for you —
Please tell me "yes" or "no" if you want it.**

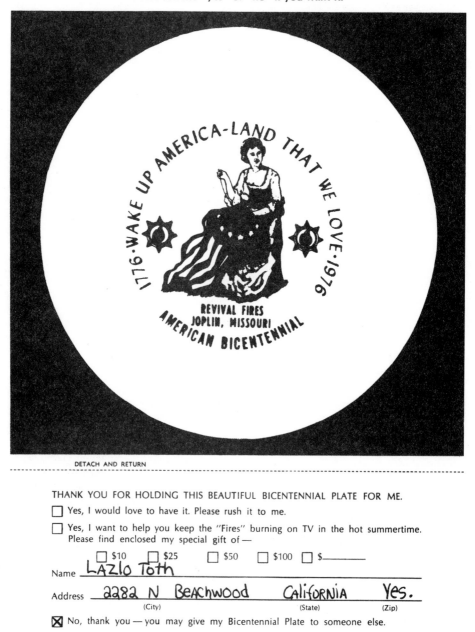

DETACH AND RETURN

- -

THANK YOU FOR HOLDING THIS BEAUTIFUL BICENTENNIAL PLATE FOR ME.

☐ Yes, I would love to have it. Please rush it to me.

☐ Yes, I want to help you keep the "Fires" burning on TV in the hot summertime.
Please find enclosed my special gift of —

☐ $10　☐ $25　☐ $50　☐ $100　☐ $_____

Name **LAZLO Toth**

Address **2282 N Beachwood**　**California**　**Yes.**
　　　　　　(City)　　　　　　　　　(State)　　　(Zip)

☒ No, thank you — you may give my Bicentennial Plate to someone else.

Use this coupon to send us your Tricentennial idea.

Send your idea to:
Tricentennial
Atlantic Richfield Company
P.O. Box 2076
Los Angeles, CA 90053

From: Lazlo Toth

Address 2282 N. Beachwood

City Los Angeles **State** California **Zip** yes

My idea is:

<u>Make people talk less!</u>
It's a known fact that each human gets only two billion words.
Nobody has ever run out yet because nobody has lived long
enough. Figuring that the average human speaks about 50,000
words per day, that's only 18,250,000 per year. And even if
you live to be 100, you still would have 1,750,000 to go.
But, in the future, when people start getting transplants and
they learn how to reverse the aging process, people will start
to live to be 200-300 years old and a lot of us will be running out of words if we don't start rationing them now. So,
for the Tricentenial, I say tell the people to start cutting
down on talking.
<u>As to your other questions:</u>
<u>Best way to solve energy problem:</u> Get energy from rocks!
All day long all they do is soak up the sun rays - that's
energy we can use - let's get going!
<u>Universal language:</u> Yes! English.
<u>How can architecture of the future improve on that of the</u>
<u>present?</u> Bacements! Today (present) they're building a lot
of homes without bacements. No place to store things! Where
can you store things? Attic? No, too hot!

These are all the visions I could think of today. Together
I know we can do it!

We have always been a nation more interested in the promise of the future than in the events of the past.

Here at Atlantic Richfield we see the future as an exciting time. The best of times. And we know that all of us can achieve a splendid future by planning for it now.

We'd like your help. We need your vision. America will change a great deal by the year 2076. We want you to tell us what you think those changes should be.

What do you envision as the best way to solve our energy problems?

Should we have a universal language?

How do you think architecture of the future can improve on that of the present?

Or, if those topics don't appeal to you, pick one that does.

Please note that all ideas submitted shall become public property with-out compensation and free of any restriction on use and disclosure.

Petroleum Products of
AtlanticRichfieldCompany

Celebrate America's Tricentennial 100 years early.

August 4, 1976

Mr. Lazlo Toth
2282 N. Beachwood
Los Angeles, CA 90068

Dear Mr. Toth:

Thank you for your letter in response to our Tricentennial
Program.

By way of background, Atlantic Richfield Company designed
this program to encourage people to look ahead and express
their visions and desires for the future. Today, most people
are so deeply involved with personal affairs, they tend to
forget that our future is a public matter requiring the
interest, attention and participation of us all. We believe
that your efforts, along with those of many others, can
ultimately translate into the action necessary for planning
a better future.

We intend to publish a summary report which will be sent
to you when it is completed. This was made possible by
everyone submitting their ideas without compensation and
free of any restriction on use and disclosure.

Sincerely,

George V. Kriste
Manager

GVK:cb

NO REPLY!

SUCCESS
☆ IS MORE THAN AN ☆
EGO TRIP

Your life story. Professionally written. Book-length biography-autobiography. The ultimate personal statement. Who you are and what you have accomplished.

(Contact:) Editor-in-Chief:
Clifford Irving
Literary Developments, Inc.
Pan Am Building, 200 Park Avenue
New York, New York 10017
Suite 303 East (212) 986-2515

Mr. Clifford Irving
Editor-in-Chief
Literary Developments, Inc.
Pan Am Building, 200 Park Avenue
New York, N.Y.

Dear Clifford,

Well, I see you didn't waste your time making license plates! This life story thing is a big idea! You can make a million!
But let me give you a little advice:
They may say "ego trip" and things like that in the pen but it won't work on the men you're trying to reach now. Your idea appeals to former business dynamos who enjoy reminiscing and re-thinking their careers. They're in their late 60's and older and would not relate to your headline:
          <u>Success is more than an ego trip.</u>
I suggest your headline say:
          <u>How to live forever!</u>
That will suck them in!

Let me know the cost of having my autobiography done!
The Knights of Columbus is willing to pay for half of it but I'm not going to write nice things about them just because they're paying.
I'll want a lot of pictures in it, and figure in a color photo of my medals. Is color extra? Do you write in Spanish, too? I know you spent a lot of time over there. I think my life story would have a lot of appeal in Spain - also in Chili - and also in Greece! Could we get someone to do the Greek version? I'm too busy with my correspondence to go hunting Greeks! Hire some Turks, they'll find them!

Looking forward to meeting you and starting on the project. Let me know how much I'll be making.

                    I hope you like dogs,

                    Lazlo Toth
                    Lazlo Toth

P.S. Do you know Alejandro Royo-Villanova?
      He's from Spain! I thought maybe you
      knew him! What a coincidence!

2282 N. Beachwood
Los Angeles, California
90068 - zip
August 5, 1976

Governor John B. Connally
First City National Bank Building
Houston, Texas

Dear Former Governor Connally,

I'm mad as can be! I just heard that there are elements of
the Republican party who are trying to sabotage your plans
of becoming Ford's V.P. They're saying you once offered our
former President (Nixon) a payoff in the form of Texas oil.
What baloney! What would President Nixon do with a lot of
Texas oil? It would be too obvious to have a lot of oil in
one's garage - even if he did have a lot of cars like our former President does. You can't eat it!

I'm sick of hearing about people picking on him - and you!
You have my pledge to try to put an end to all this foul
conversation! You and President Ford will make a great team!
It will be great to have two of our former President's picks
on the same ticket! Quinnella!

Fight! Fight! Fight! I'm with ya!

                          Every Body needs you!

                          Lazlo Toth
                          Lazlo Toth

P.S.
I heard a rumor that you were Oswald's true target.
True or false?

P.S.S.
Send me a button - Connally for V.P.
I will wear it to Kansas City.

VINSON, ELKINS, SEARLS, CONNALLY & SMITH

ATTORNEYS AT LAW

FIRST CITY NATIONAL BANK BUILDING

HOUSTON, TEXAS 77002

LONDON OFFICE
47 CHARLES STREET, BERKELEY SQUARE
LONDON WIX 7PB, ENGLAND
TEL:01-491 7236
CABLE ADDRESS:VESS
TELEX:24140

TEL:AC 713 236-2222 CABLE ADDRESS:VINELKINS TELEX:762 146

WASHINGTON OFFICE
1701 PENNSYLVANIA AVENUE, N.W.
SUITE 1120
WASHINGTON, D.C. 20006
TEL:AC 202 298-5550
CABLE ADDRESS:VINELKINS
TELEX:89680

August 31, 1976

Mr. Lazlo Toth
2282 N. Beachwood
Los Angeles, California
     90068

Dear Mr. Toth:

Thank you very much for your kind remarks in
your letter of August 5, 1976. I appreciate your
support.

I am sorry to say that since I am not a candidate for the Vice Presidency, I do not have any
buttons to send you.

Thank you again for writing.

Sincerely,

John B. Connally

JBC:cs

2282 N. Beachwood
Los Angeles, California
90068 - ZIP CODE
August 20, 1976

President Gerald R. Ford
The White House
Washington, D.C.

Dear President Ford,

Congradulations on your victory last night in Kansas City!
And congrats on that wonderful acceptance speech. It was
your best by far, that's for sure!

I'm proud to see you took my advice and picked a four for
Vice President. When Roland* wrote (Monday) you had already left for the convention and he said you still hadn't
made your decision - guess he forwarded it on.
   FORD & DOLE, four and four! Good buttons! Good going!

I know you had other reasons for picking him besides the
good button reason - I understand he's a hard-hitting cam-
paigner and that he's got a well known sardonic sense of
humor. Just what America needs!

I know that this is the comeback trail for you. People
are afraid of Carter because they don't know what they're
getting, but with you they know. Keep it up!

                        72 days (yards) to go
                        until November 2!
                        Lean to your left -
                        Lean to your right -
                        Stand up, sit down -
                        Fight! Fight! Fight!

                        Lazlo Toth
                        Lazlo Toth

*
My best regards to "Roland". When I saw Sec's Simon,
Kissinger, Butz, Vice-President Rockefeller, etc. all
at the convention, I said to myself, "Who's watching
the store?". Now I know - brilliant!

September 2, 1976

Dear Mr. Toth:

Thank you for your thoughtful message following
my nomination.

Our record over the past two years is a positive
one, and I am proud of it. Our Nation has made
steady progress toward prosperity, peace and
public trust. America today is sound and secure,
confident of full economic recovery and of a
better life for all our citizens.

Our challenge is to build on this record of
achievement and I appreciate your support and
interest in sharing your thoughts with me.
With your help I know we can win in November
and continue the job that is so well begun.

Sincerely,

Gerald R. Ford

Mr. Lazlo Toth
2282 North Beachwood
Los Angeles, California   90068

2282 N. Beachwood
Los Angeles, California
90068 - ZIP CODE
August 21, 1976

Senator Robert Dole
The United States Senate
Washington, D.C.

Dear Senator Vice-President Dole,

Congradulations on being chosen to be the new Vice-
President by President Ford. I know that a man who
they call "the Kansas wit and whipcracker" will do a
good job campaigning and irking Carter while President Ford returns to being President. That's smart
politics! The best way to run for President is to be
President! That's been true since before Hoover and
it still holds water today. Carter can make up fancy
campaign songs but only the President can play <u>The Star
Spangled Banner</u>!

I'm sure glad our President picked you instead of
Reagan. I used to like Reagan but when he picked
Schweiker we got to see what Reagan (closet moderate)
is really like. For awhile I was thinking President
Ford would choose someone with more experience for Vice-
President - like William Miller. Even though he's had
a lot of T.V. (television) exposure with that American
Express commercial, it would have been a mistake. People
don't like public servants that are always charging
things. And if you loose your wallet and somebody uses
it, you have to pay up to a certain amount. Who needs it!

                              Onward to November!

                              Lazlo Toth

                              Lazlo Toth

𝔘𝔫𝔦𝔱𝔢𝔡 𝔖𝔱𝔞𝔱𝔢𝔰 𝔖𝔢𝔫𝔞𝔱𝔢

WASHINGTON, D.C. 20510

August 31, 1976

Mr. Lazlo Toth
2282 North Beachwood
Los Angeles, California 90068

Dear Mr. Toth:

Thank you for your letter congratulating me upon my
selection as the Republican Vice-Presidential candidate.

Though we will face a rigorous schedule, Elizabeth and
I look forward to the campaign and find inspiring the many
kind messages we have received from all our friends and
supporters.

We deeply appreciate your taking the time to contact us.

Sincerely yours,

BOB DOLE
United States Senate

<u>MADDOX IS THE MAN!</u>

2282 N. Beachwood
Los Angeles, California
90068 - ZIP CODE
September 3, 1976

Mr. Lester Maddox
c/o Lester Maddox's Pick Rick Restaurant
6820 Roswell Rd.
Atlanta, Georgia

Dear Lester,

I hope you don't mind me calling you Lester. I feel
like I've known you for so long I can take the liberty.
A few years back I was traveling through Georgia and
I had some bites at your restaurant. Hot beef, mashed
potatoes (good gravy), three chocolate doughnuts, and
coffee. I had my Dobermans in the car and I bought two
breaded veal cutlets (TO GO) for them. Remember me now?
How are you? I've been fine, thanks.

I'm writing to congradulate you on winning the Presidential nomination of the American Independent Party.
I read that Ford said, "The American people don't want
someone for President who they didn't know a year ago".
I'm wondering if they want someone who they didn't know
<u>two</u> years ago! That's why you have a big advantage
over Ford and Carter - you've been with us since Civil
Rights Days! Like President Ford says, "we need someone with experience". And that man is MADDOX! Lately
I've noticed in the papers that they've been getting
restaurants for using turkey instead of chicken in the
chicken salad. I just thought I'd warn you. Also, if
the coffee isn't "mountain grown" but you still have
the sign up because the last coffee was mountain grown,
take the sign down before they try to say you're trying to pull something!

I read that a keynote speaker at the A.I.P. convention
said that "<u>America's freedoms rest in four boxes</u>: <u>The</u>
<u>Soapbox</u> - <u>The Jury Box</u> - <u>The Ballot Box</u> - and, most
important - <u>The Cartridge Box</u>." He should have said
<u>FIVE!</u> How about <u>The Mailbox</u>?
If it wasn't for <u>The Mailbox</u>, how would people get to
<u>The Jury Box</u>? They wouldn't even know they had to be
there! Telephone? No! How about the people who don't
have phones and those who have unlisted numbers? Do
you mean to tell me all a person has to do to get out
of jury duty is get an unlisted phone number? Never!
Not in a FREE America! And you can do it!
And I hope that when you get elected you'll find a good
job for President Nixon (Roland). They have him busy
answering mail and things like that - and even though
it's our fifth freedom, it's degrading. How about Secretary of Health, Education and Welfare? That's what
America needs!

Lazlo

Lazlo Toth

Here's $1 so you can get America
back on the tracks of freedom!

October 25, 1976

Honorable Lazlo Toth
2282 N. Beachwood
Los Angeles, California   90068

Dear friend Toth:

I just wanted to thank you for your generous contribution of $1.00
and let you know how much I appreciate your support.

I regret to have not written you sooner, but we just received the
letter a few days ago.

As you may know we do not have federal campaign funds as our two
opponents have. They get $25 million each plus a combined $50
million or more in free news media coverage.

If you could influence others to help as you are doing, please do
so. Financial support is needed immediately for the success of
this effort. I also covet your prayers and without such support
all our efforts are in vain.

Keep up the good work and keep in touch.

Yours for victory,

LESTER MADDOX

2282 N. Beachwood
Los Angeles, California
September 10, 1976

Mars Team
Jet Propulsion Lab
4800 Oak Park Drive
Pasadena, California

Dear Mars Team, (Scientists, Engineers, Generals, etc.)

Congradulations on landing on Mars! Twice! (Viking I
and Viking II.) And congrats on inventing that terrific
arm you have for retrieving soil samples to see if life
exists there.
A SMALL SCOOP FOR A MACHINE, A GIANT SCOOP FOR MANKIND!
You can use that - get it?

From what I understand, the main experiment to test if
there is life on Mars consists of cooking the soil with
intense heat and if carbon is burned off from it - that
means there's some kind of life present.
That's where you're wrong! If carbon is burned off, that
doesn't prove there's life on Mars! That proves there was
life on Mars. You killed it!
I heard this fellow Carl Sagan say that life on Mars could
be entirely different from life here. For instance, maybe
they're real small. Maybe a whole country the size of the
U.S. was in that scoop! Also maybe small dogs were present
in that soil! How would we like it if they came down here
and started scooping up people and dogs and testing us for
carbon? We would be upset! And we would have a right to
be upset!
What I think we should do is this:
Put a small microscope in the next Viking (Viking III you
will probably call it) and take a good close look at that
soil before you go burning it.

Also, I don't like this talk about there being a canyon on
Mars that's three times larger than the Grand Canyon and
saying "it makes the Grand Canyon look like a trench". A
TRENCH?! Who said that? TREASON! The Grand Canyon will
always be the #1 canyon and no lousy pictures from outer
space are going to distort a national monument! The scenery
in the U.S. is the best! Don't go confusing people talking
about other places - especially if you can't even get there
if you wanted to go.
Question: How much would it cost for gasoline if it was
          possible to drive to Mars at present prices?
          (53¢ per gallon - regular - self serve)

                              Carry On!

                              Lazlo Toth

National Aeronautics and
Space Administration

Langley Research Center
Hampton, Virginia
23665

OCT 2 0 1976

Reply to Attn of PL-12131-GAS (264-325)

Mr. Lazlo Toth
2282 N. Beachwood
Los Angeles, California 90068

Dear Mr. Toth:

Thanks for your interest in Viking. I suggest you look at the
enclosed Viking articles in Science magazine. So far we are
still investigating the possibility of life on Mars and only
part way through the experiments.

Your idea of a microscope is one we have considered for some time
and undoubtedly will be added to a future mission.

Sorry about the Grand Canyon of Mars. It really is an enormous
feature - 3000 Km long - but I agree with you ours is still number
1. The trip to Mars is about 400 million miles. At $.53/gallon,
say 20 miles to the gallon using a compact car, the cost would be
about 10 million dollars - but of course there's no road yet.
At 55 mph, it would take about 8 million hours. That's about 10
centuries - sounds like a good trip. Bon Voyage.

Sincerely,

Gerald A. Soffen
Viking Project Scientist

2282 N. Beachwood
Los Angeles, California
90068 - ZIP CODE
September 17, 1976

President
TIMEX Corporation
666 Steamboat Rd.
Greenwich, Conn.
06830 - ZIP CODE

Dear Sir:

I saw one of your commercials that showed a woman
on the beach in Malibu, California, with one of
those ticking geiger-counter type things, and she
found a watch buried in the sand.

I lost a watch a number of years ago, and I'm not
sure, but I'm pretty sure it might be mine! I've
never been in Malibu but I figure a strong current
could have carried it down there. (My watch wasn't
a Timex, but I figure you never know.)

Could you please go through your lost and found box
and see if it has the initials "LT" on it and also
the inscription, "In case of accident call an am-
bulance".

Thank-you.

                              I also liked the one where the
                              guy's dog swallowed the watch
                              and he took it to the Vet and
                              today it's still ticking. One
                              question: How about the dog?
                              Still ticking too? Keep it up!

                              Lazlo Toth
                              Lazlo Toth

P.S. Where can I get one of those geiger-counters?
If you don't have my watch I might start looking for
it myself. Can you do any harm to a dog if you go
over it with one of those things? Any harmful rays?
Also, how about cats?

TIMEX
CORPORATION

666 STEAMBOAT ROAD
GREENWICH, CONNECTICUT 06830
CABLE ADDRESS : TIMEX GREENWICH

September 27, 1976

Lazlo Toth
2282 N. Beachwood
Los Angeles, Calif. 90068

Dear Mr. Toth:

Thank you for your letter of September 17.

We regret to advise that we do not have a lost and
found department.

Metal detectors are available through hobby stores.

Thank you for writing.

Sincerely yours,

E. David Johnson
Mgr. Market Development-Service

EDJ/ld

2282 N. Beachwood
Los Angeles, California
90068 - ZIP CODE
September 28, 1976

President Gerald R. Ford
The White House
Washington, D.C.

                    RE: THE FIRST DEBATE

Dear President Ford,

Who won the first debate? There is no doubt in
my mind who won the first debate - Gerald Ford!
The President! (The one on the right!)

My favorite was when the sound went off - that
showed him! Keep it up!

                    34 days (yards) to go
                    until November 2!
                    Lean to your left -
                    Lean to your right-
                    Stand up, sit down-
                    Fight! Fight! Fight!

                    Lazlo Toth
                    Lazlo Toth

President Ford Committee

1828 L STREET, N.W., SUITE 250, WASHINGTON, D.C. 20036 (202) 457-6400

October 8, 1976

Lazlo Toth
2282 N. Beachwood
Los Angeles, California   90068

Dear Mr. Toth:

Thank you for your recent letter expressing support for
President Ford. We appreciate your interest since kind
letters such as yours give us encouragement as we work
towards victory in November. The concern and enthusiasm
of millions of Americans is indeed an invaluable contribution to the campaign.

Since taking office, President Ford has done much to
overcome the many problems facing America. His firm
leadership and sound policies have led to an increase in
employment, a decrease in inflation, a heightened prestige
abroad as well as a renewed sense of peace and prosperity
here at home. The President looks forward to his next
four years during which he can continue to provide the
vision and strength to ensure a brighter future for all
Americans. As President Ford stated in his acceptance
speech on August 19, 1976:

> While I am President. . .we will build
> an America where people feel rich in
> spirit as well as in worldly goods.
> We will build an America where people
> feel proud about themselves and about
> their country.

Thank you once again for your message of support and I
hope that President Ford can count on your vote in
November.

Sincerely,

JAMES A. BAKER III
Chairman

The President Ford Committee, James A. Baker III, Chairman, Royston C. Hughes, Treasurer.

2282 N. Beachwood
Los Angeles, California
90068 - ZIP CODE

Mr. Charles H. Stanley
President - J. Edgar Hoover Fund
5 Bel Air
North Little Rock, Arkansas

Dear Mr. Stanley,

I just read in the paper that you are trying to
raise half a million dollars to build a monument
for J. Edgar Hoover. At first I didn't know where
I could write you, so I called Little Rock information (501) and got your address from them. I
just hope you're the right one!

It sounds as though you're going to have some
statue and I just hope it can be done before the
Bycentenial is over. It would only be fitting!
That's for sure!
Mr. Hoover did many wonderful things for this
country - watching over our safety from Communists,
etc. - and all the presss (the extra s is for soc-
ialism) talks about is how he got people who were
working for him to mow his lawn and fix his clogged
drains and that stuff! Enough!
Why do they try to discredit the best people we
have? First President Nixon, and now Mr. Hoover!
(And they used to do the same thing to President
Hoover - no relation.)
Thank you Jesus we have someone like you to show the
other side of the coin and build a statue!

Enclosed find $1 American to do my share for freedom!

                         Stand by our flag!
                         Fifty states - one God!

                         Lazlo Toth

                         Lazlo Toth

J. EDGAR HOOVER MEMORIAL FUND

4422 Ellicott Street, N.W. • Washington, D. C. 20016

October 29, 1976

Mr. Lazlo Toth
2282 North Beachwood
Los Angeles, California 90068

Dear Mr. Lazlo:

　　Thak you for your letter and kind remarks
about Mr. Hoover. We, too, feel he did many wonderful
things for our Country.

Sincerely,

Charles H. Stanley
5 Belair
North Little Rock, Ark.

To: *Lazlo Toth*

The J. Edgar Hoover Memorial Fund, sponsored by
the Society of Former Special Agents of the F.B.I.,
Inc., acknowledges, with gratitude, your contribution to this fund.

RALPH H. JONES
Society President

Date *November 9, 1976*

Amount $ *1.00*

Sponsored By The Society of Former Special Agents of The Federal Bureau of Investigation, Inc.

NO REPLY !

2282 N. Beachwood
Los Angeles, California
90068 - ZIP CODE
October 6, 1976

Sec. Earl Butz
Dept. of Agriculture
Washington, D.C.

Dear Former Secretary Butz,

It sure is a shame that just because of a joke
during a personal conversation with John Dean and
Pat Boone you have to resign your job!
Not long ago in Illinois they made the Pekin
Chinks change their name to the Pekin something
else, and now this thing with you! When are
they going to leave us alone!

I was wondering - did John Dean or Pat Boone have
any good jokes to tell you? I was thinking maybe
Pat Boone had some jokes to tell about Arthur Godfrey. Did he say anything about why Godfrey fired
Julius LaRosa? That's been on my mind for some-
time and I'd like to get to the bottom of it.

GOOD NEWS: When my alarm clock radio went off this
morning (5:30), what song do you think was playing?
A song entitled The Duke of Earl!
Coincidence? Some people would probably say "yes",
but I think it was probably a sign that means better things are in store for you! Maybe now would
be a good time (astrologically speaking) to try
that joke out on The Gong Show. You never know!
If you'd like, when you come out you can stay at
my place. I'm pretty busy, working on the campaign,
but I think I'll have time to show you around.
Farmer's Market - first!

Keep campaigning for President Ford! You are a real
asset to his campaign, that's for sure!

                        Forward with Ford and Dole!
                        Four and Four!

                        Lazlo Toth

                        Lazlo Toth

P.S. Last night on the Tonight Show, Johnny Carson
said, "It's for sure Butz won't be picked to host
Soul Train." He's got a nerve throwing stones at
you - I understand that The Great Carnak is really
him!

2282 N. Beachwood
Los Angeles, California
90068 - ZIP CODE
October 13, 1976

President Gerald Ford
The White House
Washington, D.C.

Dear President Ford,

<u>Who won the second debate?</u> That's a good question!
Some say you won it ("President Ford won it"). And
some say Carter won it ("Carter won it").
My personal opinion is - <u>DRAW!</u>

I think you would have had him if you didn't get into
that "Eastern European countries are not under the do-
mination of the Soviet Union" stuff! I understand that
a lot of Eastern European stock are upset because you
said that - and they have a right to be! If those countries are so free, how come they're all stuck over in Eastern
Europe instead of where the weather is better? I wouldn't
feel like voting either if I had to stand in line in the
cold for six hours! Come on!

My friend George Tuttle (Polish American) say's you probably got some bad information from Coca-Cola lobbyists or
people like that who just want to go over there and make a
fast buck. Don't listen to those types! Listen to Roland!
And from now on I think you should stick to saying things
you've said before. They might jump on you for repeating
things but you won't get into any hot water that way. Make
a rule - <u>No New Thoughts!</u>
I'll try to swing Tuttle's vote back to you - I think I
can do it.

                          19 days (yards) to go
                          until November 2!
                          Lean to your left -
                          Lean to your right -
                          Stand up, sit down,
                          Fight! Fight! Fight!

                          Lazlo Toth

                          Lazlo Toth

    P.S. I saw your commercial that showed you talking
          with a lot of kids - it was great! Move over
          Bill Cosby!

Dear Friend:

President Ford will be visiting cities
and towns across our country during the
closing days of the campaign, and he
regrets very much that he cannot respond
personally to your recent letter. He has
asked that I write and thank you for letting him have your views on some of the
important issues facing our Nation.
Because citizens across America share
many of the same concerns, I thought you
might find of interest this copy of the
President's remarks at a recent campaign
stop.

With the President's best wishes,

                Sincerely,

                Roland L. Elliott

                Roland L. Elliott
                Director of Correspondence

Enclosure

OFFICE OF THE WHITE HOUSE PRESS SECRETARY
(Raleigh, North Carolina)

_____

THE WHITE HOUSE

REMARKS OF THE PRESIDENT
AT THE
NORTH CAROLINA STATE FAIRGROUNDS

12:17 P.M. EDT

Governor Holshouser, Liddy Dole, Dave Flaherty, distinguished officials and guests:

It is great to get together with one of my family again, our third son, Steve Ford.

I also wish to express my deep appreciation for the fact that an old and very dear friend of mine, Congressman Jim Broyhill, is here.

For many, many reasons, it is a great privilege and a very high honor to be back here in the Tarheel State, and I thank you for the wonderfully warm and hospitable welcome.

In Kansas City, I promised not to concede a single vote or a single State. I meant it, and let me give you where I have been to prove the point. Some people have said, well, I have been spending my time in the Rose Garden. Some people have been saying I have been hiding out. Well, here is the itinerary.

Today I was in Virginia, now in North Carolina, and later in South Carolina; last week in Oklahoma, Texas; the week before in Louisiana, Mississippi, Alabama and Florida. I don't think that is hiding out in Washington, D. C. (Laughter)

A couple of weeks ago I opened up the State Fair in Texas, but Jim Holshouser told me if I wanted to see a really big fair, I would have to come to North Carolina. I am here and I love it. Thank you.

Well, while I am here, let me extend a very special invitation to come to Washington next January for the inauguration of Jerry Ford and Bob Dole; or, to put it another way, you all come. (Laughter)

(OVER)

2282 N. Beachwood
Los Angeles, California
90068 - ZIP CODE
October 15, 1976

Mr. E. David Johnson
Mgr. Market Development-Service
TIMEX Corporation
666 Steamboat Rd.
Greenwich, Connecticut 06830

Dear Mr. Johnson:

I find it almost unbelievable that a company your
size and in your business doesn't have a lost and
found department. Where do you put all the watches that people find? You must have some department
where those watches are funneled through! Who's
got the watch that was in the commercial?
I guess you thought it was a good story but didn't
care about the person who lost it and gave you the
reason for doing that commercial in the first place!
Don't get me wrong, I'm not saying that it's mine -
I just don't think you should go and make a commercial about a person's loss and then have everybody
profit from it except the person who made the whole
thing possible!

Also, I checked at three different hobby stores and
none of them have metal detectors! You said that
metal detectors are available through hobby stores
and they're not! What gives? The way I figure it,
if you can't expect a watch company to be organized,
who can you expect? Since you make so many watches,
everybody may be carrying around the wrong time! For
all we know, it could be later than it really is!
Does anybody really know what time it is?
And I don't think you should brag so much about how
many watches you sell. Remember, if "MORE PEOPLE
BUY TIMEX THAN ANY OTHER WATCH IN THE WORLD", more
people must lose Timex than any other watch in the
world, too! I'm not saying you have to go around
telling people that more people lose your watch than
any other watch in the world, but I don't think you
should brag about how many you're selling and only
tell half the story. Maybe you could say something
like: IF YOU FIND A WATCH, CHANCES ARE IT'S TIMEX!
I give you this slogan FREE!

If you'd like, I think I could organize a lost and
found department for a company your size. I have a
lot of experience in that area and could start the
first of the year. We can do it!

Keep TIMEX #1!,

Lazlo Toth

Lazlo Toth

TIMEX
CORPORATION

666 STEAMBOAT ROAD
GREENWICH, CONNECTICUT 06830
CABLE ADDRESS: TIMEX GREENWICH

October 29, 1976

Mr. Lazlo Toth
2282 N. Beachwood
Los Angeles, Calif. 90068

Dear Mr. Toth:

Thank you for your letter of October 15, 1976.

As we are sure you can appreciate, watches lost by
consumers generally are found by individuals that
return them to police stations, etc., not to the
manufacturer. Accordingly, we do not maintain a
consumer lost and found department. We will, however,
consider your suggestion of creating such a department.

We regret that you have been unable to find a metal
detector. In the east, they are sold by hobby stores.
Perhaps you might look in the yellow pages under "metal
detectors" to find a dealer in your area.

If we can be of further assistance to you, please notify
us.

Sincerely yours,

E. David Johnson
Mgr. Market Development-Service

EDJ/ld

2282 N. Beachwood
Los Angeles, California
90068 - ZIP CODE
October 21, 1976

General George Brown
Chairman of the Joint Chiefs of Staff
The Pentagon
Washington, D.C.

Dear General Brown,

Just a few lines to let you know that there's one
American out here who's proud and honored to have
a General like you as our Chairman of the Joint
Chiefs of Staff. Navy, Army, Air Force, and Coast
Guard all under one roof and one man! And that man
is you! A man named Brown! Keep it up! And keep
our country number one! If we let our national de-
fense down, we might as well give Russia the keys
to Cincinnati! Say goodbye to Proctor and Gamble!
People will ask the stores, "What kind of soap is
available?", and they will say, "Only one kind, the
communist brand". Is that what they want?
And the same types say, "NO!" to the B-1 bomber!
"NO!" to underground testing! "NO!" to killing
Whales! What's next? Will they be telling us, "NO!
you can't go to the church of your choice?" Never!

And I'm sorry to see that you're in a little hot water
over a comment you made about Israel.
Accusations (shrapnel of the press) fly - but remember, "names can never hurt you".* But, when shrapnel
is flying you've got to remember to STAY LOW! Anybody
that's been to the movies knows that!
Also, regarding what you said a few months back - I
don't know anything about Jews controlling all the
banks and newspapers, but I know for sure one area
that they seem to control completely - Deli's! You
don't have to be Columbo to figure that out!

Keep doing a good job and stay true to our President!

Keep our flag on top!

Lazlo Toth
Lazlo Toth

* from the poem Sticks and Stones,
  author unknown.

OFFICE OF THE CHAIRMAN
THE JOINT CHIEFS OF STAFF
WASHINGTON. D C 20301

13 December 1976

Mr. Lazlo Toth
2282 N. Beachwood
Los Angeles, California 90068

Dear Mr. Toth

This is to acknowledge your recent letter to
General Brown.

He wanted me to convey his appreciation for
your words of support.

Kind regards.

Sincerely

JOHN C. CONLIN
Colonel, USMC
Staff Assistant

2282 N. Beachwood
Los Angeles, California
90068 - ZIP CODE
October 25, 1976

President Gerald Ford
c/o The White House
Washington, D.C.

RE: THE LAST DEBATE

Dear President Ford,

Congradulations! Maybe you didn't <u>win</u> the third
debate - but you didn't lose it either, which means
<u>VICTORY IS OURS!</u>
The way I figure it, you're only a few points behind
now and with $4 Million to spend in the next week,
there's no stopping you! Like President Nixon says,
"the tube is where it's at!". You can blitz the big
states and come November 2, they won't know why, but
they'll be pulling that lever named "FORD". The last
word is all that counts! People are afraid of the
unknown - and that's why you're going to win!

<u>A SUGGESTION:</u> It's not too late - I just heard a song
on the radio that can guarantee your election: <u>Hold on
to What We've Got</u> by Frankie and the Four Seasons. Buy
it, and put it with pictures of you campaigning! It
can do it for you!

Also, one more suggestion: I think you should stop
calling Watergate "the lonely national nightmare". It
wasn't lonely! You and President Nixon and the rest
shared it with all of us! It was like a <u>group</u> nightmare.
Also, I don't understand, if it's "settled once and for
all" like you keep saying, why everybody keeps talking
about it! They already forgot about your Eastern European remark, why can't they forget everything else? Nuts
to them! Remind them that your dog's name is "Liberty".
All the other Presidents just had dogs named like dogs,
yours is named after a human right - and everybody knows
dogs aren't human. I don't know what that proves exactly,
but it's something to use when they start bringing up Watergate! They won't know what to say!

8 days (yards) to go
until November 2!
Lean to your left -
Lean to your right -
Stand up, sit down,
Spend! Spend! Spend!

Lazlo Toth

Lazlo Toth

THE WHITE HOUSE
WASHINGTON

Dear Friend:

President Ford will be visiting cities
and towns across our country during the
closing days of the campaign, and he
regrets very much that he cannot respond
personally to your recent letter. He
asked that I thank you for your support,
and let you know that he appreciates your
thoughtfulness in sending him your views.

Your help will assure victory on November 2
so that under President Ford's leadership
our Nation can move ahead with confidence
into our third century of freedom and
liberty.

With the President's best wishes,

Sincerely,

Roland L. Elliott
Director of Correspondence

2282 N. Beachwood
Los Angeles, California
90068 - ZIP CODE
November 3, 1976

President Gerald Ford
The White House
Washington, D.C.

Dear President Ford,

The returns are in and you are out - and I can't
believe it! Demand a recount! There must be some
mistake! How can the American people elect a man
President who they don't even know instead of a
proven leader? You gave us the win pin, you pardoned
President Nixon, you protected us by all those vetoes,
and this is how they repay you? I'm moving! They did
the same thing to President Hoover and now they're
doing it to you! I should have moved then!

I think our biggest mistake was the fumble during
the second debate. We never fully recovered. And
Butz, General Brown and Dole (King Weasel) sure didn't
help! But I really thought all the money saved for
the last quarter would pull us through. It goes to show
you - those people that say money is the only way to
win elections are full of beans (lima)! Send them back
to Peru! I've had it!

I just heard that they shipped the dummy of you at
Madame Tussaud's Wax Museum to storage (next to Nixon)
in the basement. I bet if they ever do a remake of the
movie House of Wax you might be in it! You see, some
good always comes from the bad! Also, when they make those
plates with all the pictures of the Presidents on it,
you will be among them! Hundreds of years from now, you
will probably just be glumped together with all the Presidents wearing ties (like we glump together all the Presidents with beards), but those in the know will say, "Ford,
he was a good one!".

Will you be moving out to San Clemente, too? I was wondering - do Liberty and King Timahoe know each other? It
sure would be wonderful if you could mate them! How about
a puppy? Female only! My dobermans will kill a male -
they're real picky when it comes to being around other dogs!
But it sure would be an honor to have an offspring of you
and Roland!

You did a good job, Jerry!
You played a good game!

Lazlo Toth

Lazlo Toth

NO REPLY!

2282 N. Beachwood
Los Angeles, California
90068 - ZIP CODE
November 20, 1976

Ambassador Leornard Firestone
Ambassador to Belgium and President of Nixon Foundation
Brussels, Belgium

Dear Ambassador Firestone,

I wondered why I never heard from you, not even a thank-
you, after I sent you some money for the Nixon library -
and now I see President Ford is spending a vacation
(laying low) at your place on the 13th fairway of the
Thunderbird golf course in Palm Springs. Is that anywhere
near Frank Sinatra's place? I hope not! I heard that
Agnew spends so much time there that the whole neighborhood
smells like Baklava. I hope the smell doesn't get in the
way of our President's strokes. That's all he needs!

Well, now I know why you didn't write back - you were
made an Ambassador! Congradulations! Any chance of stay-
ing on with Carter, or will you be going back to running
the library full time? Next stop, Akron?

I think it's kind of interesting that just two days ago
I got two new tires for my car and today I saw a right-up
about President Ford unwinding at your desert home. I got
a flat a couple of days ago and the guy (bob) at the
station (ARCO) said he couldn't fix it because the tire
was worn down too much and it wouldn't hold a plug. So I
got two new ones since the other back tire was pretty worn
down, too. I didn't know if I should have gotten new ones
or not - it's a '62 and I don't know how much longer I'll
be keeping it. I don't see why they just can't put tread
marks right in the cement instead of always having to get
new tires!

My suggestion: Why not combine the Nixon library with a
Ford library and save the American people some money? It
can be a monument to the 8 years of the Nixon-Agnew-Ford
epoch. And why not put it right there on the 13th fairway
in Palm Springs? It seems like a perfect place!

                        It's all over now!
                        It looks like this
                        is THE END,

                        Lazlo Toth

                        Lazlo Toth

NO REPLY !

2282 N. Beachwood
Los Angeles, California
March 28, 1977

The Honorable Carl Albert
Former Speaker of the House of Representatives
Bug Tussle, Oklahoma

Dear Honorable Sir:

I just read where you said you could have stolen
the Presidency if you wanted to! You said you
could have kept Ford out of the Vice Presidency -
and then you would have been next in line when
President Nixon resigned!
And I also read the kind remarks you made about
President Nixon. That was nice of you - considering
you were on the other side. But I think you would
have gotten in there and continued President Nixon's
best policies and done a great job! "President
Albert" they would have called you - and whenever
the Presidents of the U.S. would be in alphabetical
order you would be right up there with the two
Adams! Right before Buchanan! (Where you belong!)

One question for history - If you had become President, who would have been your ideal choice for
Vice President?

Thanks for not making Watergate any
harder on us than it was - but I
think we would have been better off
with you!

Lazlo Toth

April 1, 1977

Mr. Lazlo Toth
2282 N. Beachwood
Los Angeles, California 90028

Dear Sir:

I have just received your very nice
letter of March 28, 1977. Thank you
very much. I appreciate your kindness.

Sincerely,

Carl Albert

CA/bb

About the Author

Lurking not far behind the typewriter
of the mysterious crusader and super-
patriot, Lazlo Toth, is his prayer partner
and spelling consultant, Don Novello.

Novello is also known as Father Guido
Sarducci, the gossip columnist for
L'Osservatore Romano, the Vatican newspaper.

Originally from Ohio, he presently lives in
northern California.